TIDE OF TIDES

By the same author:

Poetry

Collected Poems (1950-2011)
Trembling Man (with Juliet Holmes à Court and Ruth Levine)

Fiction

Storia Patria

TIDE OF TIDES

Poems
2011–2024

PAOLO TOTARO

RECENT WORK PRESS
2015-2025
10 YEARS OF POETRY

Tide of Tides: Poems 2011-2024
Recent Work Press
Canberra, Australia

Copyright © Paolo Totaro, 2025
Introductions © Theodore Ell and Alice Loda, 2025

ISBN: 9781764106818 (paperback)

A catalogue record for this book is available from the National Library of Australia

All rights reserved. This book is copyright. Except for private study, research, criticism or reviews as permitted under the Copyright Act, no part of this book may be reproduced, stored in a retrieval system, or transmitted in any form by any means without prior written permission. Enquiries should be addressed to the publisher.

Cover image: 'Ocean Clouds Horizon' by 춘성 강 from Pixabay
Cover design: Recent Work Press
Set by Recent Work Press

recentworkpress.com

To Patrizia

Contents

Introduction: Paolo Totaro's thirteen years of afterthoughts   xi
  Theodore Ell

Towards a poetics of togetherness: Paolo Totaro's verse   xxi
  Alice Loda

I

Un sogno / A dream	3
Building blocks	6
First time at the cinema—Naples, June 1944	9
Gary Cooper—Naples, June 1945	10
Opera theatre	11
Baronìa d'acquisto / Peerage for sale	12
Cinque giornate / Five days	14
Giornata prima: Cos'è un idillio? / First day: What is an idyll?	16
Seconda giornata: Il Tratturo / Second day: The old sheep track	18
Giornata terza: Cos'è il Parlamento? / Third day: What is Parliament?	22
Giornata quarta: L'astronomia / Fourth day: Astronomy	26
Giornata quinta: Lo spazio / Fifth day: Space	30
Name days	34
Mamma's teacups	36
I wanted	37
Love, yes	38
A quality of daring	39

II

Capire / To know	42
Empires	46
Trojan Women	48
Speaking of war	49
We them (aka Volunteer)	52
The art of war	53
Il primo Ulisse / The first Ulysses	56
A gentle answer / Una calma risposta	60
The hungry, the thirsty, the stranger	62
Gods' obituary	63
Seeking asylum	64
Bureaucrazies	65
Immaginario / Imaginary	70
Saints	80

Runaway bride	83
Lament	84
Sentinel	85
Antiche bombe e il Coronavirus / Ancient bombs and the Coronavirus	86
Mandela	90
Disimparare / Unlearning	94
Ginger	96

III

Illogical digressions from serious present-day matters	98
The question	100
The art of self-deprecation	101
… And foundering is sweet in such a sea	102
You asked me	103
Áccent accént	105
Evolution's true crown	106
Middle ages	107
What is a cow?	108
Danny Lovecraft	109
The country of *hmm* and *like*	110
Funneling the nation	111
Fence sitters	112
Asymmetries	113
Space semiotics	115
To make tea	117
Nested riddles	118
Misquoting Shakespeare	120
New Year's Eve litany of fears	121
Miti sinistri / Universal logic	122

IV

A lesson	128
Free-fall	129
Come Lui li volle / As He wanted	130
Parola e logos / Word and Logos	132
The bees	134
A wailing sonnet	136
House hunting	137
Lyrebird	138
Wallaby tracks	139
The birth of myths / Il nascere dei miti	140
Tribunal: Hearing at dawn	142
Closure	143
Non sequitur	144

Pittwater	146
Le colline dormono ormai / The hills are now asleep	150
When sails are born	152
Spare a thought	153
Like Argos	154
Funeral for a wallaby	156
Deep-wading	157
House lifting	158
Tide of tides	159

V

Come di sera d'estate / As on a summer's evening	162
Carpe Diem a Balmain	166
Elkington Park: The thriller	168
Homeless	169
Afternoon at the Art Gallery of NSW	172
En attendant Juliet	174
Lost in translation	175
Nosferatuner	176
Utilities	177
The new Pope / Il nuovo Papa	178
Rumour	180
Canberra Press Club	181
Eye vision	182
It catches up with us	183
Stockpiling	184
Gifts: contemplations	185
The gift of cowardice	185
The gift of delusion	186
The gift of self-deception	187
The gift of fire	188
The gift of grace	189
Un regalo gradito / A gift appreciated	190
One old woman	194
If you publish a book	196
At the gym	197
L'arte del conversare / The art of conversation	198
Cena domenicale / Sunday dinner	200
Patrizia at sixty	202
Idyll	203
The day the internet died	204
Fidelio	205
C'è un'ortensia in giardino / There is an hortensia in the garden	206
Aminya Place	208

Sisters	209
Mail stone	210
And as I sit docile	212

VI

Trembling man	216
Hospital corners	217
Ulysses	218
Quando / When	220
Esodo / Exodus	222
Eternal feminine / Donne eterni Dei	226
Stop listening / Smetti d'ascoltare	228
Tu mi dicesti / You told me	230
Primavera / Springtime	232
Oltre tanti io, una gente / Beyond many I's, one crowd	236
Inventario / Inventory	240
Finire logicamente / Ending logically	246
Serenità / Serenity	248
Contest / Gara	250
Fork in the road	254
For a faraway child	255
An age of unsteady progress	256
Eulogy for Kim Gamble	257
The race	258
Delayed clarity	259
The architect's gene	260
Ave atque vale	261
Ecce gratum	262
Pygmalion	264
After the deluge	265
Open the door	267
The quest	269
Sombrement	270
Last prayer	271

Introduction:
Paolo Totaro's thirteen years of afterthoughts

Theodore Ell

Paolo Totaro's *Collected Poems* were published in 2012. The poems in that volume numbered upwards of a hundred. They were written initially sometimes in Italian, sometimes in English, and in many cases presented in both. Taken together, the *Collected Poems* constituted the work of more than sixty years, spanning the period from 1950 to 2011—'all my adult life,' as Totaro wrote in his foreword.[1]

Except that there was, and there is, more life to come, and with it a startling concentration of poems. In the thirteen years since his *Collected Poems*, Totaro has written as much poetry as he did in the sixty preceding years. This new book collates that remarkable yield, together with some uncollected or revised poems from earlier times.

In so doing, this book belies the preoccupation of many of the poems with infirmity and impermanence. For every presentiment of mortality or every shift of feeling towards resignation, there is a counterpoise, perhaps an observation or intuition or aphorism, or simply an expression of mood, which refreshes the poet's sensitivity to a vital spark. For all the eclecticism of this volume—Totaro's wit, the breadth of his intellectual interests and the variety of his expressive modes are undiminished—its chief motive is an insistence on life for life's sake. The composition of the poem 'I Wanted,' drafted in 2012 and revised in 2023, spanned the main period represented in this book, and the finished item puts the poet's case clearly. Thinking back to Naples in the 1930s, Totaro remembers himself as a boy glorying in imagination and wanting to achieve daring and fantastical feats. The poem then returns us to the present, or more precisely to 2023, with Totaro at the age of ninety and, despite frailty, finding his boyhood instinct undimmed. He writes, 'It's a fact. I still want.'

The drama of this collection lies in the difficulties of acting upon and enjoying that 'wanting' to live, when so much that was inherent and familiar about life has changed, not only beyond recognition but also sometimes, it seems, beyond reality.

The poet's problem is not only that the body changes, though the physical difficulties of age become an increasingly important theme as the poems proceed. It is also that experience threatens to narrow and fray apart. Emotional connections drift out of reach with the loss of friends, anxiety grows inwardly at the thought of leaving behind habitual and beloved places, and time itself, no longer filled with the same activity and momentum as it was in the world of work, dilates and meanders in many directions. Implicit in most of these poems is a sense that life is slowly being emptied of its contents ('Monday Tuesday ... Saturday Sunday, / each a withdrawal from your stock'—'Aminya Place'). Yet even if material is infinitesimally ebbing away, experience is by no means vacant. On the contrary: these poems reflect insights that are new to Totaro's work. The poetic impulse reconnects with experiences and presences buried beneath the adult memory, and even suggests that some presences believed to be long gone may have circumvented and overtaken the present and now lie ahead, waiting for the poet to rejoin them. In particular, memories of the poet's late father Giuseppe Totaro (*'babbo'*) acquire a second dimension, as in all the factual lessons *babbo* taught him as a child the poet seems to perceive another latent and inchoate lesson: that to resign oneself in silence ('a pause between one unspoken word and another'—'Cinque giornate' / 'Five days') is to reconcile oneself to pain. It is a lesson that the poet senses he was too innocent to realise at the time, but that he may at last be at the threshold of understanding.

The imminent resolution of old mysteries is made possible thanks to a new sense of completeness, or near-completeness, in the self. This, more than anything else, represents a fundamental departure from the *Collected Poems* of 2012.

In his essay 'Participation—a poetic perspective,'[2] which introduced that volume, Gaetano Rando rightly characterised Totaro's migration from Italy to Australia in 1963, and its repercussions in Totaro's subsequent careers in business, academia and government, not least as the head of the New South Wales Ethnic Affairs Commission from 1977 to 1989, as the central psychologically and thematically determining element of Totaro's poetry. The social, political, emotional and linguistic difficulties of the migrant experience lay at the centre of the poetry's reckoning with the Australian setting. This preoccupation was conveyed emphatically in such poems as 'Multilingual Exercises,' a sequence which blended vocabulary and idioms from numerous migrant languages to convey the migrant's difficulty in expressing the huge effort of adapting to new life in Australia—with the ironic result that the patois of migrant words, at first glance nonsensical, succeeded in conveying a communal testimony as a mosaic builds an image from dissimilar fragments. 'The difficulty of saying things that really count,' Gaetano Rando wrote in his essay, 'is perhaps another way of expressing that participation in the culture of the adopted country is a no less wistful aspiration than past participation in the culture of the country of origin.'[3] That is to say, in Totaro's poetry up to 2012, to be a migrant was to be twice removed and twice yearning, negotiating a bewildering new life via ideas and language that belonged to another life seemingly beyond recovery. In contrast to these agonised social concerns, Rando also rightly presented Totaro's experience of coming to know the Australian landscape and natural environment as an essentially happy one. One important element that maintains continuity between the *Collected Poems* of 2012 and the new poetry published here is Totaro's retreat at Pittwater, a tranquil inlet off Broken Bay north of Sydney, which exists in the poetry, then as now, as 'an idealised oasis of peace,'[4] in Rando's words.

Even if the settings of many of the new poems are familiar, in this new collection the theme of migration, as the poetry had conceived it since the 1960s, has all but vanished. Now, the sense of dislocation, the presence in the self of a great rift or contradiction, and the incessant imperative to adapt to equally incessantly strange surroundings, have diminished into far lesser significance. References to or memories of migrant matters do sometimes arise or may be implicit in the background; there is, after all, no denying or ignoring the immense fact of migration or its effects on personhood and self-definition. '[I]n the experience and testimony of the migrant,' the Australian historian Alistair Thomson has written, 'migration never ends.'[5] Thomson was commenting on the experience of certain migrants who had returned to live in their country of origin, for whom migration had constituted a huge and painful detour in their lives. Totaro's past poetry acknowledged and accommodated the possibility of such pain, but now the pain he himself felt is not nearly so acute. The division between Italian life and Australian life, or the Italian self and the Australian self, effectively has become merely notional and is no barrier to the imagination. The process of adjustment is either complete or redundant; the sense of alienation has worn away. These new poems travel backwards and forwards between the Italian and Australian situations of Totaro's experience and find equally rich symbolic potential in both.

The collection opens with the lyric 'Un sogno / A dream,' in which Totaro's *babbo* returns to visit him, not so much from the dead as from the aftermath of an interrupted dialogue which both father and son have been hoping to resume. This surprising but welcome visitation ushers in a series of poems in which scenes of childhood in Naples, including memories of wartime in the 1940s, come vividly to life in the present, as Totaro goes about life in suburban Sydney. The longed-for but inhibited dialogue between father and son, broken off by migration, as represented in 'Conversazioni mute' / 'Mute conversations' in the *Collected Poems* of 2012,[6] now opens to full imaginary expression. Quiet reminiscence is magnified into a full re-living of events. The Italian part of life and the Australian part, each as fully evolved now as it can be, are speaking on equal terms across a lifetime's distance. Totaro's migration has indeed never ended, but it has evolved beyond its initial form as a schism in experience and identity, to constitute instead an enlargement of both.

One other essential distinction between this new poetry and the *Collected Poems* of 2012 is the shift in Totaro's perspective on, and feelings about, the 'oasis' of Pittwater. Totaro's attachment to Pittwater is as imaginatively nourishing as ever. In the moods of water, the minutiae of the shoreline and the lives, deaths and habits of animals ('the worms drilling into pylons, / [...] the blue soldier-crabs / immersed in their writing on the sands'—'Tide of tides') the poetry is just as ready to find symbols for human feeling. Yet for that very reason, in these new poems there runs beneath the veneer of peace a strong undercurrent of unease and anxiety. Whereas once, as Gaetano Rando perceptively suggested in 2012, Pittwater 'perhaps mirror[ed] a conscience disturbed by the tension between a wistful aspiration to interior peace and the reality of social conflict,'[7] now it mirrors a conscience disturbed by awareness of its own finitude and a fear that the cherished things it will leave behind may not endure. At one level, the poet has changed and continues to change irrevocably, while Pittwater, on the timescale of nature, appears changeless. At another level, darker and deeper, the poet suspects that when Pittwater does change—as a heating climate and rising sea levels seem to dictate it must, its timescale being unnaturally hastened—then it will consume and wash away everything Totaro had thought, hitherto, would outlast him. 'Will these paintings float?' he asks,

> Will these chairs remain anchored
> to the convivial table?
> And this ream of paper, will it be toy to waves
> and feed to plankton?
>
> 'Tide of tides'

These questions may be nervous but if they entail an absence of certainty, let alone of hope, then the conclusion of 'Tide of tides' indicates they need not also entail despair. Once, Totaro took comfort in the notional fixity of Pittwater as a haven from work and politics. Now, he takes comfort in the notion of passing through Pittwater, as before him Indigenous Australians did, in a transaction whose ultimate balance and meaning the haven itself will calculate:

> Earth is ageing. These bays age,
> this old beach saw the ritual feasting.

>[...]
>...the oscillations of the moon, like of taste,
>sweep away bad and good
>but hand back any overdue payment
>in the fullness
>of astronomical time.
>
>   'Tide of tides'

'Interior peace' now is a matter of learning the lesson of renunciation suggested inscrutably by the *babbo* figure. Whether it is to be achieved through meditations on the hugeness and cyclical character of natural time, as in the new Pittwater poems, or through negotiation with the elusive and querulous figure of God himself, as in a number of poems that dramatise debates (and disputes) over God's mixed ethical record, these new poems reach one by one towards the possibility that peace and reconciliation may indeed be at hand. There is no submission to a higher being; rather, a higher being, whoever or whatever it is, may be persuaded to submit to the poet's point of view. 'Cammina, cammina lento, lento con me / verso la fine del temnpo e del sentiero,' the poet enjoins ('Walk, walk slowly, slowly with me, / towards the end of time and of the path'—'Finire logicamente' / 'Ending logically'). With every step along this path, footsteps become lighter and shapes disappear. It is the poet, not the formless companion he invites to join him, who is the guide on the way out of material life.

The capacity to envisage such peaceful shedding of the self and its burdens is hard-won. Before the poems turn to these reflections in earnest, the collection pauses to deal with harsh moral questions raised by the opening sequence of childhood memories of war. The descent of ever more countries into disastrous war in the opening decades of the Twenty-First Century has preoccupied Paolo Totaro with the same ethical intensity as the social status of migrants, many of them refugees from war, did in the late Twentieth. As in his testimony, political and poetic, of migrant experience, so in his poetic condemnations of war and warlike speech and behaviour, Totaro's ideas are shaped fundamentally by personal experience, having witnessed bombing, famine and disease in Naples between 1943 and 1945. 'Is this really the end of hell?' he remembers wondering, as a boy, of eventual liberation and peace ('Building Blocks, I'). Perhaps as a series of events in his life it was, but just as in the mind the migration never ends, neither really does the war. Contemporary war is essentially identical to wars of a lifetime ago: 'Sono i vecchi che capiscono la guerra' / 'It is the old who know what war is' ('Capire' / 'To know'). The distress of traumatic memories haunts the sleep of the elderly but also, in Totaro's depictions, erupts beyond sleep as a waking nightmare at the outbreak of each contemporary conflict. Expressions of pity for those who suffer give way to barbed satirical denunciations of the ethical lapses that make war possible. At the peak of this sequence, God himself stands accused. God's self-serving and evasive defence is a blunt inversion of the lament of the crucified Christ: 'Man, why hast thou forsaken me?' ('The Art of War').[8] Why, indeed, when in Totaro's view, the permission of war must stem from God's 'eternal solitude, / unpossessed of man's capacity / for carnal love?' ('The Art of War') Here is another source of Totaro's anxiety about what might happen at the end of life. God, at this stage in the collection, seems uninterested in having human souls for company.

Small wonder, then, that the poems of war are demarcated from the rest of the collection with a body of comical and experimental pieces, almost all of which qualify for the title given to the first in the section: 'Illogical digressions from serious present-day matters.' Light-hearted manipulations of form, humorous gifts to fellow poets: amid all his reflections on ageing and haunting memories since 2012, Totaro has also mined a rich vein of whimsy, the climax of which is his proclamation of Neapolitan pizza as the 'highest crown' of all evolution.

Yet the comedy cannot last in full flight for long, with the concerns of age weighing as they are on the poet's mind. There is, he senses, something 'sinistro / così assai sinistro' ('sinister / so very sinister'—'Miti sinistri' / 'Universal logic') shadowing the merrier moments. As soon as we leave these 'illogical digressions' behind and return to 'serious present-day matters,' the sinister feeling becomes pervasive. The death of a much-loved Moreton Bay fig tree in a neighbourhood park is a puzzling shock. The poet wonders uncomprehendingly, with a repressed desperation, at the stark reality of so much teeming and insistent growth coming to an end: 'The fact is the Moreton Bay tree now / is dead and we don't know why and I / for one am truly afraid of inquiring' ('A lesson').

It takes the remainder of the collection for the poems to find the means to 'inquire.' It is this process, which unfolds through the second half of this book, which constitutes Totaro's main endeavour in poetry in the past thirteen years, and which has brought about the changes in his outlook and themes. Each poem in the second half of this collection marks a small realisation, a reality of age and transience faced, articulated and, in a sense, mastered. The earliest achievements are acts of recognition, expressed uncomplainingly and with disarming simplicity: 'It catches up with us, no matter what, / That tiredness of life,' the poet is forced to admit ('It catches up with us'). Gradually, recognition accumulates into familiarity: 'Walking these streets you sense a void. / [...] You know the void will reappear tomorrow morning' ('Aminya

Place'). At last, there is acceptance, as the encroachments of age and mortality focus appreciation on what life there is left:

> The cup is not full to the brim.
> Leave time
> for the overflow
> and hope any addition
> to my temporal lifetime
> is a gentle one.
>
> 'And as I sit docile'

It is realisations such as this that allow poems in the closing sections of this book to voice exhortations to courage, even celebration. Poignant elegies to departed friends only further concentrate the affection addressed to friends and companions still living, not least Totaro's wife Patrizia Ravalico, as well as magnifying the love of company as an end in itself, as expressed with particular tenderness and strength in 'L'arte del conversare' / 'The art of conversation.' Company of a more purposeful kind is invoked in the poem 'Ulysses,' an allegory for the long and uncertain journey into the daunting regions of advanced age. One by one, different manifestations of the Ulysses character, the personification of steadfast desire to find a way home, come aboard Totaro's 'ship': Homer's Ulysses, or Odysseus, the cunning warrior and restless traveller; Dante's embittered Ulysses, forever damned for exploring beyond the divine boundaries of the known world; Tennyson's stoic Ulysses, the wearied but still hardy old-timer; Joyce's 'Ulysses,' or rather Leopold Bloom, the character who rummages deep in the messy modern soul; and NASA's Ulysses space probe, the ultimate in precision wayfinding. Their companionship is not a spur to heroism or triumph, but to face the unknown, 'this voyage of very last release,' in a spirit of open-mindedness.

A similar ethic inheres in 'Trembling man,' which gave its title to an exhibition of artworks and poems in which Totaro collaborated with artists Juliet Holmes à Court and Ruth Levine in 2017.[9] This short and gently ironic poem presents itself as a showman's announcement, reconceiving the affliction of Parkinson's disease as the kind of prodigious stunt Totaro dreamed of accomplishing as a boy:

> I am the trembling man.
> I tremble therefore I am.
> If the diagnosis is correct
> will a Doppler effect
> be my fuzzy main trait?

> Slow but secure
> I shall become a blur
> a blear a mist a haze
> and people will amaze
> because, trembling man,
> alone I know where I am.

This poem ushers in the collection's closing stages, in which the last vestiges of sinister feeling are soothed away, even if melancholy and wistfulness remain. What the poems are contemplating, after all, is the prospect of an entire life approaching its close.

Not yet, one suspects. Not yet—not while there is still the impulse to articulate poems. Totaro's notional 'entire adult life' of poetry has already enjoyed an extension of a full thirteen years. Although this book is complete, his poetic instinct is undiminished. I would not put it past him to write a good deal more.

This collection has not only been assembled at Totaro's behest but also collated, arranged and edited with his full assent. I have had the good fortune to know Paolo Totaro and Patrizia Ravalico since my childhood. Later, having grown up to poetry, I had the happy opportunity to publish new poems of Paolo's, including some collected in this book, in the journal *Contrappasso Magazine* between 2012 and 2015. In the following years, I knew that Paolo was writing many more poems, but also that he was reluctant to assemble a new collection. He was keeping the poems in reserve until he sensed they had accumulated whatever collective meaning was implicit in them. It was exciting, early in 2024, to hear from Paolo that he felt the poems had reached their watershed—and it was an honour to receive his invitation to collate and edit the volume and to translate about a dozen new poems that existed only in Italian.

During a conversation with me and Patrizia in their dining room at Aminya Place, Riverview, in Sydney, Paolo handed me the new poems as a sheaf arranged in alphabetical order by title. This arbitrary order was intended to render each poem self-contained and separate from the others, so that, as editor, I might read each on its own terms and catch resonances and affinities between poems independently of Paolo's ideas. It was in reading them privately, then grouping them by theme or mood (at one point spreading them out on the floor of my study), that the line of gradual acceptance of transience, and the access of peace, became evident to me—and it was a thrill, not to say a relief, when Paolo said his and my impressions of the poems' intentions matched. Readers may, naturally, read the poems singly or in any order they choose, dipping in and out, but this collection is deliberately arranged to present a certain arc of feeling from beginning to end.

This phenomenon, the drama or 'narrative' of across the six sections of this volume, exists independently of both the initial alphabetical arrangement and the poems' chronology. Paolo has recorded the years in which the poems were written, and reading them in chronological order would be a worthwhile critical endeavour, to see in what sequence the poems' ideas evolved. Strict chronology, however, would not reflect the experience for which Paolo has been reaching. He has undertaken the intellectual and emotional reflections expressed here many times over; only at certain moments has he been able to set certain aspects of the experience down in poetry, and even then haltingly and out of sequence. This is why the book has taken thirteen years to find its shape. The 'narrative' order reflected here is a reconstruction of a long and difficult philosophical process which, most of the time, has felt beyond words, but for which, one by one, words have been found nonetheless.

Paolo Totaro has always written in both Italian and English and many poems in this book exist in both languages, with Totaro having translated himself in both directions. Where a poem exists in both languages, the original language appears on the left-hand page and the translation on the right, but readers should not assume this always means Italian will be on the left and English on the right—sometimes English came first, and sits on the left, and Italian followed, and sits on the right. Indications of who translated which poem can be found at the end of this book. My translations are fairly conventional reflections of the original Italian poems, but it is essential to explain that in several cases, when translating himself, Paolo transposed sense but not structure, elaborating the target language into a slightly looser or tighter form, to explore different possibilities for rhythm and density of meaning. Of some examples, it could even be said that he has written the same poem in two languages at once, his poetic licence being legal in both jurisdictions.

In my English translations, I have tried to be simple, emulating the unaffected and gently matter-of-fact qualities of Totaro's own statements and voice, while maintaining an equable tone and smooth contours of sound. My editorial interventions have been limited to occasional minor adjustments in punctuation or lineation, and then only to clarify who is speaking when, or to ensure fidelity to a poem's established pattern. I have refrained from 'correcting' certain English formulations which might seem anomalous or unidiomatic, such as certain lines of 'Trembling man,' 'people will amaze / [...] alone I know where I am.' The phrase 'people will amaze' is probably a literal rendition of the Italian reflexive verb *stupirsi* conjugated in the third person future: *si stupiranno*—literally, 'they will amaze [themselves],' not literally the same as the passive Enlgish 'they will be amazed' but, in Italian, entirely the same in sense. And for the closing line, the formulation 'I alone know where I am' might seem a more conventional and rhythmically fluent rendition than 'alone I know where I am.' Yet there is nothing 'incorrect' about these or similar utterances in the English poems. They are Paolo Totaro's idiosyncrasies as a native Italian speaker and fluent English speaker still capable of occasional slippages between the two languages. Such glitches in code-switching are as intrinsic to his voice as whimsical metaphors, pithy quips or lucid emotional description, and were they edited into a conventional idiom the poems would end up sounding nothing like him.

    I am deeply grateful to Paolo for placing his trust in me to assemble this book, as I am to Patrizia for her kind, generous and equally trusting support, and to Alice Loda for so willingly joining us and for her contributions to wider understanding of Paolo Totaro's work in a fuller context. It has been a privilege to assist Paolo in doing justice to what, at times, must have been a trying endeavour, philosophically and emotionally, but one at which he persisted in the belief that it would succeed poetically.

Canberra, August 2024

Towards a poetics of togetherness: Paolo Totaro's verse

Alice Loda

The Albanian-Italian poet Gëzim Hajdari described his practice of writing poetry in parallel in Albanian and Italian not as a mere act of multilingual expression but as the slow and progressive development of what he defines as *'una lingua doppia'* [a double language], a language grounded in multiplicity and that—rooted in lives and histories—irradiates his poetic imagination with a novel, powerful light.[10] When examining the works of Australian Italian poet Paolo Totaro, we witness a similar dynamic: generative encounters between languages, stories, histories, and lives happen before verse takes form on the page and inform the substance of his lines. These encounters reflect a far-reaching dialogue between fluid, emplaced subjectivities—human and non-human, individual and collective trajectories.

Contemporary poetry is a multilayered, multifaceted, high-density scenario marked by profound diversity and experimentation, even more so when it involves translingual imaginations. Totaro is a poet who is able to both expand and transcend the confessional dimensions that often foreground translingual verse, offering the reader a corpus of work marked by a constitutive and ongoing transformative nature and a transhistorical view. Centring history—fluidly conceived in a constant dialogue between different scales, from the relations of humankind with God to the tragedy of colonisation, the secret life of trees and rivers, and the mysterious and moving dance of birds and sea creatures—Totaro's poetry brings into dialogue different geological eras, places marked by antipodean distances, the souffle of winds that travel oceans, the curiosity of wanderers, the power of myths, the wonders of nature, counterpointed by the daily struggle with the sharp, cold reality of bureaucracy and politics, to which the poet reacts with irony and sarcasm. All presences, particularly those that are small and twilit (*crepuscolari*), become the centre of meaning-making and life. They are embraced and cradled by Mother Nature, whose wonders are constantly revealed by subtraction and through attentiveness—manifested in the resurfacing memory of a child, the unexpected visit of a cockatoo in the family's garden, the shadow of a fig tree whose death was unannounced and whose gifts shall not be forgotten.

Mother Nature feeds her offspring with the sweetest nectars, nourishes them with the sharp and primordial energy of the summer sun, shakes them with wind and ice, and offers to those who can truly listen glimpses of beauty in the smallest things and acts. In Totaro's poetry, wanderers are reminded that the deepest meaning of our brief passage on this planet is to keep our eyes and hearts open, to exercise care, to be able to play, to be surprised, to believe, *nonostante tutto*.

It is well known that Totaro's professional commitments and exemplary leadership have been extremely impactful in Australia in advancing social justice, supporting marginalised, migrant, and multilingual communities, and inviting participation.[11] This commitment continues in *Tide of Tides: Poems 2011–2024*, a collection that must be read in sequence with his earlier anthology *Collected Poems (1950–2011)*,[12] to which it represents a necessary complement, like a new symphony modelled around a familiar *partitura*. The musical metaphor is not introduced by chance, as Totaro is indeed an accomplished pianist. His polyhedral talent also extends to the visual arts, photography in particular, and all the seeds of this transmedial sensitivity are planted and bear fruit in this book. A priority accorded to rhythm and the ability to develop a photographic gaze consistently emerges from his verse. Totaro's investigations and observations across landscapes, subjectivities, histories, and languages are nourished by continuous reverberations of the past into the present—lived and imagined experiences that mingle in the poetic word, human time and non-human immemorial time constantly brought together in the cycle of life and knowledge. The frequent references to the theory of evolution, the insistent reflection on the beginning and future of humankind, the terrors of war framed as an exercise in self-destruction across millennia, the exploration of what remains after our transit and what role poetry has in determining this, and the investigation of the porous boundaries between beings and generations—between what is lived, what manifests itself materially, and what is imagined or remembered—bring me to assert that this book is, first and foremost, an investigation of the beyond, of what happens in the secret liminal space that opens when there is enough room for silence to rise: a book about the *oltre*.

The collection is divided into six acts, or movements, that do not trace a chronological development but rather identify poems connected by subtle yet resilient threads. Stylistically, it contains all the ingredients of Totaro's composite, sharp, photographic, fluid, and playful verse: a metre that plays with canonical and formal modules (the sonnet, the quatrain, the triolet, the rich apparatus of rhymes, assonances, anaphora, personifications, metaphors), that may become extremely essential, and that is able then extend itself into *poèmes en prose* without losing its rhythmical vigour. It is the word of a listener; hence, it embraces with energy nominal syntax, ekphrastic inserts, lists, a de-structuring and recomposing of the layers that make up the matter, foregrounding the ability to use both a magnifying lens and a telescope within the same verse. Conscious that there will be many ways to travel through such a rich and honest nucleus of poems, I propose an analysis that starts from its inner music, its structure. For my investigation, I will then follow the book's *partitura* in movements and proceed by organising my reading notes by each of the six sections, identifying for each one what I feel is an overarching word-heart.

One: Wave

In ways similar to the poet Fabio Pusterla, Totaro plays with different scales of history, encapsulating his observations within the history of humankind itself and what precedes it.[13] In his verse, we perceive an attraction to the border and to what will remain after the passage of histories and beings. This transhistorical perspective permeates a book where memory acts as a kaleidoscope and provides access to new worlds. Past and present mingle, with the former returned alive and vibrant on the page. This overarching attitude is demonstrated in the first movement, which allows us to enter the profoundly dialogic nature of the collection.

Two major presences agitate the page here: on the one side the key figure of the *padre*, who gives the poet access to the earth and the sky, the life of planets, the secrets of non-human animals (the *mezzadro*'s dog in particular), the ability to become a traveller in a connected world; on the other side, as a powerful counterpoint, the horror of wars, which is seen mostly through the purest eyes of children, past and present. This section interrogates what happens after the passage of these two powerful energies. If the dialogue with the father is not interrupted by death—his desk now in Australia, his *lessico famigliare* entering the poet's verse untouched—war itself is a repeating process, a never-ending one, a threat that travels from antiquity to the present day, tangled at the core of each being, the fear experienced ineliminable, impossible to unlearn.

As such, the eruption of Vesuvius after bombardments, the image of Frankenstein, the silence in an opera theatre once opulent and then bombarded, the quiet across the mother's teacup and her beloved ashes secretly held in the sweetness and peace of an Australian home, all drive attention to what lies beyond, to what resists in time and what returns to remind us who we are.

In this context, the wave emerges as a key image, a powerful reminder of the connection of all matter, a hint of the attraction for an overseas land, a mirror of the nostalgia and amazement a journey brings, but also, and more crucially, a reminder of cycles we are all immersed in: what we observe today, we become tomorrow. These aspects are condensed in the dialogues with the father that take form in the long poem 'Cinque giornate / Five days'. The poem embodies past-present scenes where the lines of physical time and space are so porous that they become indistinct.

> [...]
> *Ed ogni onda porta di sé ragion sufficiente*
> *e tiene viva e desta l'immaginazione*
> *ad aprirsi e parlare. Ed a pulsare,*
> *come fa questo mare, avanti e indietro,*
> *scintilla ed ombra, ombra e scintilla*
> *nel suo dialogo con la roccia bianca,*
> *i ciottoli così ben levigati,*
> *coi granchi ed i cauti paguri bernardi.*
> *E allora?*
> *È solo un idillio. Ma c'è tanto di questo,*
> *vero nei posti in cui, da cui, per cui fluisce, stando, il mare.*
> *Ma di questo, figlio, parliamo un altro giorno.*

> [...]
> And every wave brings sufficient reason with it
> and keeps imagination alive and awake
> to open itself and speak. And pulse,
> as this sea does, forward and back,
> glitter and shadow, shadow and glitter
> in its dialogue with the white rocks,
> the pebbles so finely polished,
> with the crabs, the circumspect hermit crabs.
> *So what?*
> It's only an idyll. But there's a lot in this,
> it's true in places in which, from which, through which there
> flows, as it stays still, the sea.
> But of this, my son, we will speak another day.

Like a wave, the poems of this section tend to expand and retract rhythmically, following the hills, fields, flowers, little fish, turtles, children, trees, dogs, and waters that they observe. They are moved by a familiar, almost ritual symphony created through assonances, alliterations, rhymes, and repetitions. The wave represents a return to communal history, to what makes us alive.

The form of *idillio* derives from Giacomo Leopardi's Canti, and the intertextual dialogue with Leopardi and his models (Virgil, Lucretius, Vico amongst others) is extremely pronounced in this section, as well as elsewhere in the book. Within this intertextual trajectory, we can locate the reflection on nature—mother-stepmother—engine of daily wonders and witness to the deepest pains, energy that establishes what remains, what is transformed, and what is forgotten or can't be forgotten.

Two: Silence

The second act exists in strict continuity with the first. Here, the poet returns to the memory of the war—lived as a child in Naples—and opens his verse to embrace a reflection on empires, the brutality of dictatorship and colonisation, and the impossibility of forgetting. His fears as a child in the 1940s are retraced in the eyes of children in Gaza and Syria, unwitting victims of a present that they live but will be impossible to understand or let go of. As such, the faraway, fading memory of the father who digs the poet out of dust and rubble in *The Art of War* becomes a powerful reflection on humankind, on the impossibility of speaking and protecting, and the impossibility of not feeling.

> [...]
> Did you, my then young father,
> really dig me out of dust and rubble?
> Did you unclutch my little hand
> from hers forever?
> It was never spoken of again
> and I cannot say how
> pain came to be so much a part
> of who I am and won't be again.
> The orange grove stands, undisturbed.

Extensive references to Trojan women, Homer, the Bible, Shakespeare, Dante, Mandela, Saviano ground this journey in a search for lost words, which cannot be accomplished, the journey being the word itself. The reflection on the impossibility of difference between beings—at our core, we are all the same, we are life—is embodied in the frequent appearance of Ulysses (*us*) as Nessuno (*us*) and in the dichotomy of we/them, which is tellingly recomposed as a We. We are *the other*, our enemies, the birds in our garden, the crabs that we will become again, eventually. The lines speak strongly about the evidence of a common history of beings, an encounter beyond experience itself.

This work of tapering to find connection, to reach the bone of knowledge and experience, is mirrored by the essentiality of the diction in many of the poems in this section. Verse here makes space to accommodate different and meaningful forms of silence, and only through silence is meaning found and explored.

Three: Word

One of the most evident elements of Totaro's poetry is the adherence of poetry to the reality of things and the refusal of the mantle of the poet-prophet. Poetry is completely de-mystified and reconnected to many human experiences. An extension of the act of observation, a glimpse that crosses senses and imagination to condense on the page, poetry is reworked with a patient *labor limae* until its purest, essential form is carved and achieved.

The third section of the book is dedicated almost entirely to a reflection on poetry and the word as tools capable—or incapable—of transforming into pure form. It is not by chance, then, that in this section the most visual and concrete selection of poems sits, and the metrical modules become regular, with a frequency of rhymes and isometric structures. As is common in his work, the poet uses irony to describe his work as a *passeur* and to de-mythologise the act of writing and his own identity as an author—Shakespeare himself, in dialogue with Totaro, suggests: 'Quote me, son, but earn that right' (in Misquoting Shakespeare).

Texts here are marked by a formal virtuosity that is never a pure rhetorical exercise but rather accompanies the reflection on what we can do materially with the words we are given and what powers poetry does or does not equip us with. Why do we speak, and for whom? What distinguishes our act of writing from the dance of the wings of a cockatoo in our garden at dawn? The reflection on the more-than-human and our role in the brief passage on Earth becomes central in poems such as The Question.

> There was once a monkey who asked *who am I?*
> The answer was not one that would satisfy.
> Some time later he climbed down from her tree,
> looked at the sky and asked *pray, who am me?*
> If the four words seem grammatically incorrect,
> they posited a question that took time to reflect.
> Later still, not the monkey but her descendants
> reset the question—*what is our why, our essence?*

In this section, the play on languages (dialect, English, Italian, Arabic, Spanish, Greek, amongst others) and increased human and more-than-human dialogism enables the poet to explore the power—of lack thereof—of words. The art of word-making and poetry-making, which qualifies humankind and poets, is here reclaimed by nature, rivers, crows, rocks, monkeys, hawks in place of humans. On the page we find the evidence in the remains of the process of observation, the rigour of the lines that conceals the anxiety of the question, and the disenchanted irony which characterises those who can truly access *words*, and know and accept their powers and their limits.

Four: Attentiveness

Totaro's poetry is an act of epistemological eversion, what in Italian we would call *estroflessione*. The fourth section of the book is where this quality emerges with the most disruptive, breathtaking strength. Here, we find the entire catalogue of recurring non-human allies, which make their mark on the page, participating in the act of *poiesis*: the Moreton Bay fig, the oak, bees, goannas, wallabies, lorikeets, lyrebirds, dolphins, egrets, crabs, seagulls, parrots, bats, cormorants, and octopuses. They all contribute to designing the symphony in which we are all immersed; they convene together to explore the border.

In their grace and in their death, the mystery of existence—its beauty, its cruelty, its commonality—is explored through a process that does not bring rage as its outcome, but peace. From our allies, we should learn how to die, how to transform ourselves to become life and life again. The kinship across beings that characterises this section is epitomised in the image of the lyrebird, which, like the translingual poet, can capture voices and return them but may not truly possess any one of them.

> Here is a lyrebird whose specialty is to bark
> when I call out for my dog to please come back.
> Lyrebirds own no one language. They borrow
> from whomever is closest to their very fine ear.
>
> Myself? Owned by two, or is it three, tongues
> and an infinity of inner callings and sounds,
> I move unaware of which is the voice
> and how it feels to be in possession,
> firmly, of what I might call my truest language.

In earlier studies, I have argued, drawing on the work of Aaron Moe as well as Frederike Middelhoff and Sebastian Schönbeck, that the incursion of these non-human allies in Totaro's poetry defines an eco-zoopoetic quality in his verse.[14] This quality is foregrounded by the exploration of liminality. What human qualities can we find in non-human beings? And what of them can we find in ourselves? In Totaro's poetry, the ecological figure of personification concurs in exploring this *limen*: as such, the forest becomes an orchestra, and the music produced by trees is also a way for us to approximate the tree, to feel its pulsation. This encounter is investigated in the re-adaptation of Virgil's

Georgiche, which we find in the poem *The Bees*, where the allusion to the Vitruvian bee condenses the more-than-human alliance, and where the bees are observed in their ability to build life, travel silence and absence, and be reborn from the very death of other beings. The reference to Virgil bridges the alive landscape of Pittwater in this section with myth, the golden age, and the childhood of humanity in a Vichian sense.

The pathway toward a more-than-human reflection is pursued in a poetic, intellectual—never intellectualistic— way, with multilayered verses that open up to multiple levels of sense and interpretation. Beyond the exploration, the quality of attentiveness becomes a moral imperative to perceive, the key to realizing that 'History, unlike dampness on a hot windy day, / is never a thing of the past' (in Closure).

Five: Fading

I have discussed above how Totaro's poetry works by subtraction to reach the core, the essence, and the secret of matter. Conceptually, the fifth section of the book is marked by the image of fading—not, or not only, as disappearing, but as getting to the heart of sensual experience and reappearing on the other side of the tangible, in a different form. These pages perhaps explore with greater directness the feeling of impermanence in our passage and the changes that embrace us all—which is a generative process.

As such, losing eyesight becomes an occasion to find form differently, to play on the page, to return to the dance of flying fishes and possums, to contemplate friendship and love, to give space to a crepuscular melancholy, to feel peace in our own vulnerability, to transform rage, disappointment, and fear into something that speaks to us, something that makes us feel alive once more. It is hence not by chance that Horace and Dante are the prevailing intertextual interlocutors in this section. The loss of eyesight does not prevent the observation of how the Earth is our sister, and no remnant evaporates or becomes redundant in its secret cycle.

> *C'è un'ortensia in giardino, che ha fiorito   fedele all'estate.*
> *Si è offerta nei colori sia azzurro   che pallido rosa*
> *al capriccio di un'aggiunta di aceto   o di bicarbonato.*
> *C'è anche una vasta pianta di zucca   che viaggia ed esplora*
> *preceduta da fioroni imperiali   giallo verde-nero,*
> *e tante altre piante, tutte nutrite   dal sangue, dalle ossa,*
> *dalla polvere delle vite buie   di tanti animali*

There is a hortensia in the garden, flowering loyally to the summer.
It offers itself in colours, not only azure but pale pink also
on the whim of added vinegar or bicarbonate.
There is also a huge pumpkin plant travelling and exploring
preceded by imperial clarion flowers yellow green-black,
and so many other plants, all fed on blood, on bones,
on the dust of the dark lives of so many animals.

Life that has transformed itself is observed through the memory of children who today are not at play in the garden. Yet, they were, and the imagination of them in the present is still vibrant, still holds the same consolation. The space accorded to silence is greater in stillness, but fear is replaced by the ability to feel, to transform, to become something other, something greater.

Six: beyond

The last section is the one that embodies with the greatest directness the overarching theme that travels through the book: the opportunity of the *oltre*, of what lies beyond us. It is in this section that Ulysses returns, together with reflections on loss, love, listening, and the vertigo provoked by the figuration of an impossible flight. The poems move toward an imagination of the after. What awaits us after the deluge? What will remain and what will be transformed? What of us will be forgotten? Love becomes the prism through which the remains emerge, and it is a love directed toward creatures, friends, the adventures lived and imagined, and the lover who manifests in the book as the sweetest figure, full of a grace that nourishes.

The image of the poet traveling on an old train reminds us all that we are here for no more than a brief ride, and that what remains of us is the good we have done, the pains we have lived, the wind that powerfully has filled our sail. And it is a journey worth exploring, to the end. We are no more than the mouse that patiently builds his house to protect his offspring from the terror of the world, no more than the bees that allow us to become. And poetry is nothing more than a sculpture lying in us, ready to be carved and returned to the world to which it belongs.

There is no conclusion possible to this analysis and perhaps to this book; hence I will conclude these notes with the same verses the poet chooses to seal his exploration. In the hope that we may believe, that we may travel just enough to understand, find peace, and make peace.

Last prayer

… imagine the last second of the very last minute
and, in it, the closing thought: I see your face
sculpted not in marble but in streams
of mountain water,
in the light mist that closes this wintertime

in the pink cloud that heralds
the timeless night,
in this flash that extinguishes thought.
You are.

You do not guide and are not guided. You are no further
from me than me, nor as elusive as another's mind.
And as this day

will not fade into another, I know you cannot be good
or evil. You are. You are the vessel of the serene idea
that imparts meaning to planets and stars,
to the parliament of men and to my children,
and to this raw flesh

that is your creation. Yet, it is not your grace that eludes
but our will. And this is what I feel
and that in this last second of the endmost minute
I must let go. The time to be at peace with you has now begun …

Notes

Introduction: 'Paolo Totaro's thirteen years of afterthoughts'—Theodore Ell

1. Paolo Totaro, 'Author's Foreword,' in *Collected Poems (1950-2011)* (Sydney: Padana Press, 2012), p. x.

2. Gaetano Rando, 'Participation—a poetic perspective,' in Paolo Totaro, *Collected Poems (1950-2011)*, pp. xiii-xix.

3. Ibid., p. xvii.

4. Ibid., p. xvii.

5. Alistair Thomson, 'Voices We Never Hear: The unsettling story of post-war "Ten Pound Poms" who returned to Britain,' *Oral History Association of Australia Journal* 24 (2002), p. 58.

6. Paolo Totaro, 'Conversazioni mute / Mute conversations,' in *Collected Poems (1950-2011)*, pp. 64-68.

7. Gaetano Rando, 'Participation—a poetic perspective,' in Ibid., p. xvii.

8. See Matthew 27:46 and Mark 15:34.

9. Juliet Holmes à Court, Ruth Levine and Paolom Totaro, *Trembling Man: Two Artists and a Poet* (Sydney: Padana Press, 2017).

'Towards a poetics of togetherness: Paolo Totaro's verse'—Alice Loda

10. See Gëzim Hajdari and Giulia Inverardi, 'Il poeta epico delle montagne maledette. Intervista a Gezim Hajdari', *Comunicare letterature lingue*, 7 (2007), 299–312 (p. 302).

11. See Gaetano Rando, 'Cultural Equilibriums and Linguistic Dislocations: The Poetry of Paolo Totaro." *Australian Made: A Multicultural Reader*, edited by Sonia Mycak and Amit Sarwal, Sydney University Press, 2010, 278–95.

12. Paolo Totaro, *Collected Poems (1950–2011)*, Padana Press, 2012.

13. I wrote about this quality of Pusterla's work in 'Eco-Pusterla: A Semantic-Stylistic Analysis of Bocksten', *Incontri. Rivista europea di letteraura italiana*, 35.1 (2020), 99–115 (pp. 101–08)

14. I refer to Aaron Moe, *Zoopoetics: Animals and the Making of Poetry*. Lexington Books, 2013; Frederike Middelhoff and Sebastian Schönbeck 'Coming to Terms: The Poetics of More-than-Human Worlds.' In *Texts, Animals, Environments: Zoopoetics and Ecopoetics*, edited by Frederike Middelhoff et al., Rombach Verlag, 2019, pp. 11–40. I quote these studies in '"Surging Tide at Dusk" : Translingual Poetics Between Italy and Australia', *Journal of Literary Multilingualism* 2 (2024) 190–221

I

Un sogno

Dopo un sogno dove mio padre
è riportato a casa dal vento.

Parla al vento. Gli dice, perché chiedi,
non vedi il pane impastato, riavvolto,
non senti il calore del forno già pronto?
Chi vuoi che senta cosa dici, vento?

    Siede alla sponda del letto. Attende.
    E mi sveglio, sorpreso al vederlo, lui, qui, proprio.
    Non sorride e nemmeno sussurra *buongiorno*.

Se fossi tu seduto al mio letto, figliolo, è di marmo,
soffice quanto permette l'essenza del marmo, soffice
quanto occorre a me che converso
coi morti.

È un gioco di botta e risposta
disincarnato come se tra FireWire e WiFi
soli come noi solitari voliamo
sulle ali buie di queste raffiche di vento.

    È la voce del babbo.

Perché chiedi? Vedi è solo il vento a disporre,
a caccia di calore, sottrae e scorpora e repelle.
Questa è casa, a lungo cercata e ora per nulla.

    Sogni fluttuano attorno, profumo bianconero.
    E afflati, e preghiere
    che qualcuno lassù, o forse la, più sotto,
    voglia onorare d'ascolto.

A dream

*After a dream where my father
is brought home by the wind.*

Why ask, he tells the wind,
can't you see the bread dough
being punched and kneaded,
don't you feel the heat from the wood-fired oven?
Why ask when no one can hear the question?

>He now sits on my bed, waiting.
>And I wake, surprised to see him, here of all places.
>He doesn't smile or whisper, 'Morning.'

If it were you sitting on my bed, son,
it is of marble
as soft as marble can be, as soft
as it needs be, engaged as I am in being
with the dead. It is a question and answer game
disembodied as through FireWire or WiFi
or even through our spirits alone,
as we float conjoined with wind and darkness.

>It is my father's voice.

Why ask? See, the wind has the call,
seeks heat to draw out, displace, repel.
This is home after all, long sought for and now for nothing.

>Dreams float by, breath, prayers
>that somebody up there, or is it below?
>may hear and answer.

Perché preghi? Rannicchiati, chiudi gli occhi,
arcua di più la geometria del tuo dorso,
l'ancora flessibile volontà di volere.
Gestisci i sogni come meglio tu puoi:
Sei del mondo, qui dopo tutto.
Integro alla casa che abiti. Incorrotto.

   Tale dei sogni è la vita.
   Fanno la ronda.
   Risvegliano i morti.

Non mostrano il futuro. Mascherano il passato
sotto ghirlande semplici di bianche tuberose.

Why do you pray? Curl up, close your eyes,
arch even further the geometry of your spine,
the still bendable willpower.
Manage dreams as well as you can:
You're home. Whole. Uncorrupted.

    Such is the life of dreams.
    They make their rounds.
    They awaken the dead.
    Free those who are still serving time.

Won't disclose the future but cloud the past
under plain garlands of white tuberoses.

2015

Building blocks

Age twelve I played traffic cop
to the Liberators' armoured trucks,
my thin arms saying go right ahead
but I meant is this really the end of hell?

Oh those crimson sneer breaks in black
skin veneers, redder than the sparse
geraniums flowering down lintels
bracing exposed empty door frames.

Smut of stone. Dust of night.
Recurrent curse of bombings.
Was this the first friendly drop?
Cadbury milk choc. 'You American.

You chooingum, you silk stocking,
you Lucky Strike.' Perhaps
that same day we started
breathing the DDT spray
and whitening our hair.
Farewell the sole sport of war,
addio to the calming search
for hair lice. The trucks were

end to end, for days on end,
their flow occupied the length of
Corso Vittorio Emanuele.
Snakes over that snaking way.

Corrado is unsure who they were.
He asks if the negros are from Africa
how come we call them Americans?
Soon that first day is over but the scorn
poured by the wiser children
over me silly me that plays the traffic cop
finds sounder direction.

The gaze shifts. Soon the awakened
senses of the children warn of impending
doom. Sisters. Mothers. Even other children.
Silk chocolate maybe bedsheet
sized cinquecento lire.

Down the thousand steps.
Hurry through the weekly stream
of basement doors semi-closed
The crooked vicoli. Astonished eyes
teary old men sitting out the shadows.
Vanish please vanish unfocused iridescent,
flutter of dream. Incubus.

But again and again,
as you run to school the sane smells
of the baker's oven, of the small
barber's shaving creams and of the
burning chestnuts of the street seller
had not started yet their exit. She was
a large woman the same chestnut smell
oven.

A large gown so large that she could
pee standing up and the flow would
swish under the fresh minted shoes
of the novelty soldiers. They didn't
mind. Must have been a homely habit.
Peeing.
Relieving healthy instincts
in parks, in lanes, in the basement
rooms with older women. The
children would simply sleep or fake it
in the lower bed nearby. Astute
the grandfather would keep eyes
and mouth well closed. The hand
ready to get his cut. A Lucky Strike.

2012

First time at the cinema—Naples, June 1944

Yes, we started not with Snow White but with Boris Karlóff.
We would rather take fright at one monster than scoff at seven dwarfs.

Soppy scenes with heart-shaped apple pies, birds, dewy-eyed foal
were no match for the giant man-made Man trudging to the Pole.

We were allowed to go to the nearby cinema, me and my then soul-mate.
She and I were all of eleven, intrepid explorers, but home by eight.

It was the end of bombings. But then Vesuvius erupted. The counterfeit
countervailed life's ongoing horror. Frankenstein made us used to it.

2016

Gary Cooper—Naples, June 1945

We scuttled out into daylight in awe.
Oh that winged hand, that lightning draw!

For mean-eyed strangers on the noon train
the quiet American is ready. Maybe a tinge

of evangelical certainty withholds a full smile
from the ladies. But they swoon. Such old style.

Bank, church. Sheriff, prison. Drunks, free-women.
One or two wise ladies. The young man, spurned,

ready to be the new hero. Ghosts in black and white
come now alive out in the summer daylight:

American GIs on the Lucky Strike prowl.
Nylons. DDT powder. Child, look out.

2016

Opera theatre

U-shaped, gilded and crowned,
it carried the whispered sound
of the dying soprano,
the noble baritone of a Fischer-Dieskau
up to the highest gallery rows,
where students pored over scores.

Bombed, razed by fire,
then nesting ground
to rats, bivouac to invaders,
twice reborn,
it is drained now,
wearied of any more sound.

After the ear-splitting scream
of the gargantuan tenor,
after the ritual applause,
after the last person
has shuffled out,
a golden dust softly
falls on the red velvet seats
as they consummate their love,
Silence and this late baroque,
Italian Opera Theatre.

2016

Baronìa d'acquisto

Ha nostalgia d'un passato non suo:
non suo il palazzo dal leone rampante
certo non sua l'assenza di trepidazione
al rivestirsi nella nuova sua terra

di storie custodite da altri. Porporati,
grandìose tenute, conti zii, ritratti
d'antenati, corone di ferro. Ma le fioriture
malate, la fillossera, le tenute perdute

al biribissi dal nonno pervicace
dongiovanni … Non si cura d'altro che sopire
quella parte di sè che intona il diurno

canto dell'essere poco senza quello
che nella terra antica era più lontano
della luna, ma che qui si può placare

con l'acquisto dello stemma di barone.

Peerage for sale

He longs for a past that is not his own:
not for him the palace of the lion rampant
certainly not for him an absence of unease
at clothing himself in his new land

of histories in the keeping of others. Cardinals in crimson,
magnificent estates, uncles who were counts, portraits
of ancestors, iron crowns. But the blossom
sickening, the phylloxera, the estates all lost

at *biribissi* by that pig-headed Don Giovanni
of a grandfather… No care to give now if not to soothe
that part of himself which drones the daily

chant of being not much, without that which
in the old country was farther away
than the moon, but which here can be placated

with the purchase of a baron's coat of arms.

2014

Cinque giornate

Ho mantenuto con mio padre un dialogo continuo, dalla mia infanzia a dopo la sua morte. Queste storielle di babbo che mi parla, m'insegna cose nuove, provoca la mia immaginazione, chiede mie reazioni ed io gli rispondo con poche parole, riflettono conversazioni vere e modi veri di parlare. Di tantissimi anni fa.

Five days

With my father I have kept up a continual dialogue, from my childhood until long after his death. These little stories of father talking to me—teaching me new things, provoking my imagination, asking for my reactions as I reply to him in a few words—reflect real conversations and real ways of speaking. Of many, many years ago.

Giornata prima: Cos'è un idillio?

C'è un paese di continua tepida estate,
venti gentili appena percepibili alla pelle,
alberi decidui e sempreverdi
che vivono fianco a fianco,
così che il manto dei colli e dei campi
non perde mai il timbro suo verde.
Un paese di rivoli gentili
che, dopo lento tragitto
a fecondare ogni campo, il campo di ciascuno,
e dare acqua fresca ad ogni animale,
sfociano in mare d'onda lunga
ma bassa e regolare,
vissuta di pescetti e tartarughe che volano nuotando
e squali, che si nutrono non di altri pesci,
ma di mare. E questo poi supplisce a tutto:
è cibo, feconda l'immaginazione,
riscalda, rinfresca, scambia scienza
con paesi lontani, a comprendere ciò
che c'è di là, di qua di ogni oceano.
Ed ogni onda porta di sè ragion sufficiente
e tiene viva e desta l'immaginazione
ad aprirsi e parlare. Ed a pulsare,
come fa questo mare, avanti e indietro,
scintilla ed ombra, ombra e scintilla
nel suo dialogo con la roccia bianca,
i ciottoli così ben levigati,
coi granchi ed i cauti paguri bernardi.
E allora?
È solo un idillio. Ma c'è tanto di questo,
vero nei posti in cui, da cui, per cui fluisce, stando, il mare.
Ma di questo, figlio, parliamo un altro giorno.

First day: What is an idyll?

There is a country of endless mild summer,
soft breezes barely perceptible on the skin,
trees deciduous and evergreen
that live side by side,
so that the cloak of the hills and fields
never loses its imprint of green.
A country of gentle streams
which, at the end of slow journeys
enriching every field, every last man's field,
and bringing fresh water to every animal,
give out into a sea where the waves are long
but low and regular,
where little fish and turtles live that fly by swimming
and sharks that feed not on other fish
but on the sea. And this makes up for everything:
it is food, it nourishes the imagination,
it warms, it cools, it exchanges knowledge
with faraway countries, to understand whatever
can be found out there, beyond every ocean.
And every wave brings sufficient reason with it
and keeps imagination alive and awake
to open itself and speak. And pulse,
as this sea does, forward and back,
glitter and shadow, shadow and glitter
in its dialogue with the white rocks,
the pebbles so finely polished,
with the crabs, the circumspect hermit crabs.
So what?
It's only an idyll. But there's a lot in this,
it's true in places in which, from which, through which there flows, as it
    stays still, the sea.
But of this, my son, we will speak another day.

Seconda giornata: Il Tratturo

C'è mio padre che mi porta per mano,
che si curva, che raccoglie una conchiglia fossile
fra le tante, bianche, che uscivano all'aratro,
e che mi spiega questo larghissimo sentiero:
Era lì da secoli cioè da molto, tanto tempo.

Anche prima del nonno?
Anche prima del nonno.

C'erano questi antichi pastori, come noi,
ma vestiti di pelli di pecora che, davanti alle donne
coi bambini, passavano lenti a portare una esigua
mandria di sottomesse pecore belanti
al fresco dei monti a maggio, o al più caldo
Tavoliere di Puglia, al venire dell'inverno.

Ma se questi pastori erano come noi
perché non andavano con l'autocarro?
E perché non filavano la lana delle pecore
dopo avergli tolto la pelle?

Teneva le sue più sagge parole per me. Anche
ricordo il silenzio del babbo, e del cane Leone,
che poi era solo cane di mezzadro. Erano silenzi
attenti al riso altrui cui rispondeva silenzio allegro.
O alla stanchezza o magari al dolore inespresso
ai quali la risposta era pure silenzio, ma sedato,
più lungo di pausa fra quel silenzio e un altro.

È vero. A me, babbo e così anche Leone
sapevano parlare. Lui, con un silenzio di parole.
E, senza eco, il cane con un solo, corto latrato.

Second day: The old sheep track

My father holds me by the hand,
bends and picks up a fossil,
a white shell, one among many
uncovered by the passing plough
and he explains to me this wide
path: It's been here for centuries, that is
for a long, long time.

Even before Nonno?
Even before Nonno.

And there were these ancient shepherds,
just like us, but dressed in sheep skins
who, intent upon their path,
passed right by here
followed by their women and children
migrating their small flocks of docile
bleating sheep, towards the cool
of the mountains in May,
and back towards the heat of the Tavoliere
with the coming of winter.

But if they were just like us
why didn't they use a truck?
And why didn't they weave the wool
without taking the skins?

He saved his wisest, ever fewer
words for me. So I remember my *babbo*'s
silences, and those of Leone,
the sharecropper's dog.
They would both respond

to the others' laughter with a silent smile.
To tiredness or unvoiced
pain, their answer was
also silence, but soothing, longer,
a pause between one unspoken word and another.

It's true. Both *babbo* and the dog,
Leone, spoke to me. He
with a word-filled silence, the
dog with a single wise echoless bark.

Giornata terza: Cos'è il Parlamento?

Stranamente, comprende solo animali
cui è concesso parlare. E siamo pochi.
Ce n'è miliardi d'altri, tutti da scoprire.
Tu ci credi?
Mah, non so. Forse no.
Io penso che le anime più grandi,
quelle dei cani buoni, di pelo color miele,
che osservano tutto, che rispondono
ad ogni domanda con intensi palpiti di coda,
vanno ammesse al parlamento degli uomini,
con chi traduca i sensi della bestia-uomo
in quelli della bestia-cane, e delle altre sorelle animali.
Tu ci credi?
Forse no.
E il parlamento degli esseri umani,
esplica differenti funzioni.
Dire bugie. Dire verità velate. Dar numeri e conti della spesa.
Dire quanti siamo e come, divisi, riusciamo
a far strade che dividono madre koala
dal piccolo koala, ma che uniscono chi distoglie
alla terra il passato e chi lo aliena
in strazio di nuvola e scialo d'immondizia.
Non vorrei esagerare. Tu ci credi?
Eh, sì.
Ma il parlamento fa tante altre cosine
che un uomo solo, od una donna, non potrebbe.
Forse mentre ti addormenti, questa sera, immagina
cosa faresti se, eletti al parlamento
tu ed il cane Leone,
il cane del mezzadro,
doveste dire si o no, allo stracciare
o al chiudere le piaghe della terra

Third day: What is Parliament?

Strangely, it consists only of animals
granted the power of speech. And there are few of us.
There are thousands of others, still to be found.
Do you believe me?
Um, I don't know. Probably not.
I think the very greatest souls,
those of good dogs, with fur the colour of honey,
who observe everything, who answer
every question with strenuous tail-wagging,
should be admitted to the parliament of men,
along with whoever translates the language of beast-men
into that of beast-dog, and of all their sister-animals.
Do you believe me?
Probably not.
And the parliament of human beings,
it fulfils different functions.
Telling lies. Telling veiled truths. Giving numbers and bill totals.
Saying how many we are and how, divided, we manage
to build roads that separate a mother koala
from a baby koala, but which bring together those who divest
the land of its past and those who alienate it
into torments of clouds and sumptuous rubbish.
I don't mean to exaggerate. Do you believe me?
Ah, yes.
But parliament does all sorts of other little things
that one man, or one woman, could not do alone.
Perhaps while you are going off to sleep, tonight, imagine
what you would do, if you and Leone
the dog were elected to parliament,
Leone the sharecropper's dog,
and you had to say yes or no, to tearing open
or closing the wounds of the earth

e ritornare al tempo
dei pastori o prima ancora o prima prima ancora.
Perchè, tanto, quella è l'unica strada,
quella vera: tutto ritorna e si ripete ancora.
Come le onde?

and going back to the time
of the shepherds or further back or further back again.
Because, you see, that is the only way,
the true way: everything turns back and repeats over again.
Like waves?

Giornata quarta: L'astronomia

Ecco il babbo! Rientra con la vecchia cartella.
Il gatto miagola, corre e la cornacchia
vola dalla cornice del trisnonno
alla sua spalla ed io ancora incerto, che a lui corro.

Si ferma, un poco, a dire buona sera.
Poi si va noi quattro, nel suo studio,
apre i cassetti, due, della scrivania
(ora in Australia, ornata, nera).
e tira fuori lenti ed obbiettivi.
Poi c'è il rito dello scartare
gli obbiettivi, agro odore di paglia
dai vecchi fogli pesantemente legati
con cordicelle di canapa sativa.
Lenti convesse. Concave.
Tubi di vecchio ottone. Spiegava,
forse a se stesso, diffrazione, effetto riduttivo.

E che gioia quando, dopo cena,
nella sera serena di cielo freddo
(sciarpa per me sul vecchio cappottino)
puntava il cannocchiale
fra i tetti fino alla mezza luna.
Mi apriva a quell'arco sul confine col nulla,
a quei crateri nuotanti nell'etere nero.

Diceva, è solo specchio di sole
sui picchi delle più elevate cordigliere.
Mi lasciava mettere la manopola ornata.
tanto per le piccole mani.
Le sue, protettive, forse già col tremore.
Il gatto sapeva. La cornacchia sapeva.

Fourth day: Astronomy

Here's *babbo*! He comes home with his old satchel.
The cat meows, makes a dash and the crow
flies from great-great-grandfather's picture frame
on to his shoulder and I am still hesitant, even as I run to him.

He stops, a little, to say good evening.
Then we four head in, into his study,
he opens the drawers, both of them, of his desk
(now in Australia, ornate, black),
pulls out lenses and object glasses.
Then there is the ritual of unwrapping
the object glasses, a field-smell of straw
from old pages bound heavily together
with thin hemp strings.
Convex lenses. Concave.
Tubes of old brass. He would explain,
perhaps to himself, diffraction, reductive effect.

And such joy when, after dinner,
in the calm evening with the cold sky
(a scarf for me over my little old coat)
he would point the telescope
between the rooftops towards the half-moon.
He opened me to that arc at the edge of nothing,
to those craters swimming in the black ether.

He would say it's just the sun reflecting
off the peaks of the highest cordilleras.
He let me guide the ornate handle,
a lot for little hands.
His own, protective, perhaps already with the tremor.
The cat knew. The crow knew.

Dalla spalla, non volava, appagata.
Eppure, era quella che nel tempo reale
con pochissimi armoniosi neri battiti d'ale
avrebbe potuto più avvicinarsi alla roccia lunare.

From his shoulder, contented, it would not fly away.
And yet, it was the one who in real time
with a few graceful black wingbeats
could have got the closest to the moonrock.

Giornata quinta: Lo spazio

Noi, la luna, tutti i pianeti, gli astri,
solitudini nell'indefinito comune
che chiamiamo spazio.

Come questa stanza?
Forse un poco più grande
di queste quattro mura
ma non tanto da essere
più inimmaginabile della nostra sostanza
e di questo cielo oscuro.

Iminnanannagiabile, che non si può mangiare?
Anche così hai ragione. Non si può mangiare.
Eppure se ci pensi, quello che tu mangi è spazio vuoto.

Ecco perchè rimango sempre con la fame?
Pensiamoci assieme:
fra ogni pezzetto che compone il creato
c'è tanto spazio quanto non alla luna
ma all'astro più lontano.
Anzi oltre 'lo spazio' non c'è poi più nulla
e lo spazio è un nulla ostinato ad essere nulla

Rimango con la fame se mangio nulla ...
Perdonami. Parlo difficile stasera.

Mi aprì alla luna. Una piccola roccia.
E la terra è luna ma con acqua, per ora,
e, per ora, vita.

Non ricordo più bene. Costruisco frasi
che non potrei ricordare.

Fifth day: Space

Us, the moon, all the planets, the stars,
solitude in the communal undefined
that we call space.

Like this room?
Perhaps a little larger
than these four walls
but not so much so as to be
more unimaginable than our own substance
and than this dark sky.

Uminngenannable, you mean you can't eat it?
You're right, there, too. You can't eat it.
Although if you think about it, all that you eat is empty space.

Is that why I'm always feeling hungry?
Let's think about this together:
between every tiny piece that makes up creation
there's as much space not as far as the moon
but as far as the most distant star.
So beyond 'space' there's absolutely nothing
and space is nothing that insists on staying nothing

I go hungry if I eat nothing…
Forgive me. Talking difficult tonight.

He opened me to the moon. A tiny rock.
And the earth is a moon but with water, for now,
and, for now, life.

I don't remember well now. I construct sentences
that I cannot remember.

Per primo, mi schiuse dalle sue bianche mani messe ad ale
e mi fece volare da questo nostro mondo.

Ed ora sono pronto ad andare.
Porto le sue parole come viatico attento.

First thing, he unfurled me from his white hands turned to wings
and set me flying away from this world of ours.

And now I am ready to go.
I carry his words like a doting viaticum.

2014

Name days

In Naples, long ago

March nineteenth was St Joseph's, proclaimed
by the velvety, double-flowered stock
and the street-sellers' voices: *Vee-ole!*
The shutters would open just enough
for the old wicker basket to be lowered
five floors to the street, with the Pomeranian,
the exact amount of coins and then pulled up
with a lighter Pom and a load of velvety leaves
holding tight onto masses of white and purple *viole*
that my Dad, Giuseppe, loved for his name day feast.

Then came June the twenty ninth, the feast
of twinned Saints, Peter and Paul.
Did my Saint Paul not deserve his own day?
Was it to scrimp on holidays or was a soldier
fallen from his horse on the road to Damascus
less worthy than a fisherman who was a rock,
even if the one on which was founded
the Roman Catholic Apostolic Church?

Even stranger, on December the eighth,
the Immaculate Conception did not
celebrate Mary, the Mother of Our Lord
but one *Santa Immacolata,*
my virginal Aunt Imma's name day
and wintertime gift of one more public holiday.

Santa Martha was my mother's name day.
She smoked, played bridge, a snob, mundane
and loved her only son so much that
he flew oceans away and there stayed
remorseful on each twenty-ninth of July

and now dedicates this poem to her
with loving thoughts for what could and was not to be.

2016

Mamma's teacups

Only five left, they rest
highest in the boneyard
of dishes, the glass cabinet.
Mother's bone china cups

have taken on a meaning
well above their station
of mugs made of dirt
mixed with bone ash.

I am not ashamed at all
that Her ashes instead,
sealed in an urn, are hidden
on the deepest lower shelf.

They wait for me to find
a quiet wave that will
slowly take them to Her
Mediterranean Sea.

Such is the end of *stuff*
the chemicals that are us.
The frippery continues
to define us, long time after.

2014

I wanted

It is a fact. No one can understand
all that is understood.
Yet, I wanted to walk to the horizon
where sky meets sea
to straddle unknown and known.

I wanted to fly just a centimetre above
the hot asphalt, resting softly
my hand on the wrought iron rail
of the terrace fronting the whole
mystery of the Gulf of Naples.

I wanted to make sea and horizon
reveal how they generate each other
into this growingly inscrutable prison
of fantasy, hope and injudicious play.

I wanted my mind to displace limits.
I wanted I wanted.

I was so coherent.
Incoherence came soon enough
with humility,
and energy now on the wane.
It's night, it's a fact. I still want.

2012

Love, yes

    … try as you may, what you now hear
is perhaps the mirror on the garden wall,
or leaves as they lose shine and turn to yellow
or even those nails as they rust on
and, as senses blunt, you can see voices
lost so long ago—the notary's, the priest's,

the grandfathers' banter at the table
never seemed to stop, ascending
swift through the walls, the windows,
the external staircase repainted
with white chalk, when back from the war

and whatever you held as distinct,
sound, light, touch, scent, time, love, yes,
is now disarranged, and so is all that was sharp
in this baffling garden that won't tell what and when …

2017

A quality of daring

What will you be when grown up?
A corpse. A corpse? *That's all.*
Banter appropriate for octogenarians
started early for children of war.

The days still began with a sunrise
and nights came after the sunset.
The cock crew. The wind still
wailed and school was open

whenever it could. But the few men
spoke in whispers. Mothers
cried at times, drained
from rushing with five children

out of a windowless room
—skies on fire, blast to crash
to red scream—down into air shelters.
Ours was the Funicolare tunnel.

Slow, old men gave bread,
sips of water. A guitar.
Finally, the raid-ended siren
hooted at the new sun

and kids would rush out
for fallen unexploded bombs
too large to keep. But one day,
one said a *pomegranate!*

and he would be disemboweled
with his 11-year-old sister.

Where did it come from
that winsome hand-grenade?

Oh, spent memories. Spent daring.
Spent stanzas against any war.
War won't speak back but,
sure as the sun, it reappears.

2014

II

Capire

Sono i vecchi che capiscono la guerra.
Vecchie grinzite con scialli sulla testa.
Occhi lenti impregnati del senso di chi
è mancato ed ogni giorno di più manca.

Sono i vecchi che soffrono la storia
perché l'hanno nelle ossa, nei giunti,
nell'artrosi, negli antichi scoppi e sibili,
nel timore del telegramma giallo
con le strisce incollate, simboli occulti.

Sono i vecchi che, con paltó puliti, logori,
salgono lenti sentieri di polvere
a ridosso di baratri dove lontano
una spiaggetta bianca e mare azzurro
ricordano il rosso, a ridosso di massi
dove, nascosti, il nemico e il fratello
non udivano più la saggezza del mare.

Sono i vecchi che rivedono i mezzi
anfibi di sbarco, sé stessi nascosti
dietro il fragore delle mitragliere.

E sono i vecchi che guardano in faccia
i bimbi nuovi per distinguerne il nonno
dal colore dal tenersi su eretti o più curvi.

Si, sono i vecchi e le vecchie, che alla notte
svegliati da un antico tremore della
eterna terra aprono le finestre che danno
sulla storia e lasciano entrare nella povera
stanza cavalleria tormentosa e gabbie piene

To know

It is the old who know what war is.
Old wrinkled ladies strapped in shawls,
slow eyes which still see those gone
who are missed more as days go by.

It is the old who suffer history for they
have it in their bones, in their arthritic
joints, in night terrors of bombshells,
in the fear of that yellow telegram
with stripes glued on, feared symbols.

It is the old, neat in threadbare coats,
who slowly climb now the dusty paths
along the abyss where, far away,
a small white beach and a blue sea
are still seen as red, crowned by boulders
where, hidden, both enemy and brother
no longer heard the wisdom of the sea.

It is the old who visualize amphibian
troop carriers, and themselves hidden
behind the scream of the machine-guns.

And it is the old who look into children's
faces to recognise maybe a grandfather
from the hair colour or the posture.

Yes, it is the old who, at night,
half-awake for a timeless tremor
open windows overlooking history
and let into the room harrowing
horses and cages

di uomini e donne dalle pupille bianche
che trapassano nuvole di bianca
polvere di case crollanti e nulla frena
nulla chiude nulla spera nulla.

Sono i vecchi che comprendono la guerra

of white eyed women and men
in clouds of white dust,
as houses fall curbed by nothing,
ending nothing, but leaving still
wide empty plains of plain hope.

It is the old who know what war is.

2015

Empires

Building empires is no children's game.
Not too many ever had the skill.
Those who did, in time gave way
to the entombed, who are there still.

Mussolini was a child. His toy
revenge, for the vanquished
soldiers of the Amba Aradam.
A thumb-in-mouth Caesar's dream.

No Cleopatra for him, no hubris
for the Transalpine Gaul, a lamb
whose class-room artistry, collages
from cut-out punctual train timetables,

were soon to be halted: history
would turn over his fables
for the Abyssinian Emperor,
dwarfing Vittorio Emanuele Terzo.

Bitter lingers the stench of empires
long after demise: Belgian,
Portuguese, Spanish,
French, German, Austrian,
Ottoman, Russian, Roman.

All gone. All millions who were slain,
or enslaved, or turned coat,
or sought refuge, or simply
suffered silently, are forgotten.

What remains beside the histories
and their bias. Heroes? Villains?
For us Italians
the books of history
point to one tragic joke:
Vittorio Emanuele Terzo
re d'Italia e d'Albania
imperatore d'Etiopia.

2012

Trojan Women

Euripides' anti-war tragedy, Trojan Women, *was performed at Sydney's Greek Festival in April 2019.*

Is it only an old ploy? Don't barbarians
still prepare for war their Trojan Horses
and stuff nuclear wombs
with Marines for the final plunder?

Lit by stage lights and L.E.D. flames,
the Scamander river tonight will hear
Poseidon evoking black winds
to clog the Euboean gulf with corpses.

Now as then, "is war declared
from Gods on queens and kings?
No! War is on us, our men, our children!"
is the cry of The Trojan Women.

Unfazed by the classical names,
Tonight's audience is aware
that if thousands of years have passed,
our hearts and limbs still feel pain.

"Come out! Come out," is the stage cry,
"But don't bring only Kassandra.
Bring them all out from their huts,
the indomitable women of Troy!"

They won't be paralyzed either
by Achaean or billionaires' ruses.
All women's cries—now billions—
may again be overpowering on stage
but can they save us in this nuclear age?

2019

Speaking of war

Four legs
to travel, run
or deferentially bow.
A tail
to drum sonorous
Morse code
on timber floors.

A mouth
for mock ferocious
growling
or carrying a stick
to shake and say
I can kill!

A bouncy ball.
Squealing,
a toy bone.
Dignified eyes
to beg
and a flow
of dog effluvia
to speak
in absentia
to both
foe and friend.
The inoffensive
whiff of gas
means no more
than, simply:
Park. Go. There.

All is peace
inside dog and man
when both
share this flowing shore
and bend of bay.

But then
the true time
for you to kill
is ripe and
you must leave.
He sits subdued
wise
turned the other way.

Pass the days
greying
those who stay.
OOOO OOOO
orotund
his mouth ululates
the spell:
Don't die. I feel. Alone.
Don't let them kill.
You.

The years pass
but if you do
walk in again
he runs maybe slower
barks maybe less loud
jumps for your lapel:
Remove. Please.
He sings.
All medals.

And you maybe more tired
and him go back
to the swerve of shore
to the unceasing bend of bay.
Reattune your nose,
wake your pristine
skill to link in
both offspring
of breeds of wolves.
Speak.

Speak to each silent query
Speak to each imperceptible
gesture. Speak dog
again.
Don't be for him
the mute
god in the trenches.

2012

We them (aka Volunteer)

You said they brainwash their youth to die.
I said we pay wages to our young to die.

You said they don't really know why.
I said we don't train them to ask why.

You said they live in the Middle Ages.
I said look now who uses torture chambers.

We march with eagles as symbols of empire.
They dance to ovations of madness finger to the sky.

We make children hidden under blankets' darkness.
As in daylight we wouldn't dream to conceive.

The sunlight nurtures the terror by day.
The night moon glows red in the river

Wet waders under the moonlight's gaze.
We pushed up front from the other side.

We pulled life out of ravines of prayer.
Spit fire no more after we were laid bare.

Resigned now we join in the statehood of faith.
Unguided missiles. The foul friend of fate.

Who pays to train kids to die. God. Nation.
Get your wages now. Approaching rain

Human hood your time is up.

2015

The art of war

> *My sentence is for open Warr: Of Wiles,*
> *More unexpert, I boast not: them let those*
> *Contrive who need, or when they need, not now.*
> John Milton (1608-1674) *Paradise Lost*, Book 2 -51/53

I
Where in the space of a mind
resides the repressed wailing,
the haunting of words
that never will again be said?
Did you, my then young father,
really dig me out of dust and rubble?
Did you unclutch my little hand
from hers forever?
It was never spoken of again
and I cannot say how
pain came to be so much a part
of who I am and won't be again.
The orange grove stands, undisturbed.

II
The word is that war is commonplace,
a farce, an imperial knee-jerk,
a despot's tic, a bloodied lark
imprinting liars for names
like Siege and Blockade,
Conquest and Liberation
on human vice.
Wars have no starting date,
no clear end
yet are compelling
as the outstanding dues

owed to an unremitting necromancer:
>	millions severed limbs +
>	millions burned out eyes +
>	infinitely maimed minds +
>	unfathomable hatred =

demise of hope and belief.

III

The word is that war
is God's holy masquerade.
Migratory birds
mutate into clouds of airplanes.
Crows hold congress
over snow covered corpses.
Rigidly, men in a general's costume
travel with hearth and harem
and sip tea, in the eminence
of fortified homes.
Over world charts
pinned with tinny tanks and tiny banners
they oversee the sallies of logistical resources:
gunboats, airplanes and flesh,
brainpower and more flesh and more pain.

IV

The word is that war
is imagination at its maddest,
the pinnacle of invention.
It's where giant strides are made
in the growth of common logic.
Where man destroys the companions
given to him at the beginning
and man gives God's creation
a new meaning.

'What do you, God, think of man
and our state of living with a companion
in the company of equals?
How do you look at us
from your eternal solitude,
unpossessed of man's capacity
for carnal love?
Do you ever desire to change your state?
If you sowed
the seed of assured mutual destruction
among the people
from whom you withheld conversation,
is war the way to assert over man
your bliss of absolute solitude?
If solitude is perfection, God, you must want
us out of the way to be once again alone.'

       … do I hear:
       Man, why hast thou forsaken Me?

2012

Il primo Ulisse

Il primo Ulisse
genera altri Ulisse.
Ciascun lettore
ne diventa uno.
E diventiamo
tutti Nessuno.

L'Ulisse in me
mi cambia da re
a navigatore
ad assassino
ad albero d'ulivo
alla storia d'un naso

a una bomba
che a caso
esplode
attorno a me
a te bambino
che incide

che stampa
che intaglia
fantasmi
mostri
per la mente
nel sempre.

Ulisse non era
come tu non sei
ma forse sarai
il coltello

The first Ulysses

The first Ulysses
begets other Ulysses.
Every single reader
becomes one.
And we all
become No-one.

The Ulysses in me
turns me from a king
into a navigator
into a murderer
into an olive tree
into the story of a nose

into a bomb
which at random
explodes
all around me
around you child
who engrave

who print
who carve
phantasms
monsters
for the mind
forever.

Ulysses was not
as you are not
but perhaps you will be
the knife

che scintilla
dall'ombra
di questi versi
che sono
Nessuno.

that shines
from the shadow
of these lines
that are
No-one.

2013

A gentle answer

Which is the merchant here, and which the Jew?
The Merchant of Venice (4.1.169)

Which is the merchant here, and which the Jew?
Which is the bomber here, and which the Arab?
Which is the preacher here, and which God's voice?

Who stands for sheep here and who for wolves?
Who stands for wolves here and who for foxes?
Who stands here for life and who for thought?

What brings us truth more than a wounded child?
What brings the desert wind, the scream of whom?
True to word. True to voice. True to doubt.

You shed skin, blood, life juices, inner voices.
You cry: *Whose knife is piercing my back?*
Who is demanding a pound of my flesh?

2014

Una calma risposta

Chi è il mercante qui, e chi l'ebreo?
Il Mercante di Venezia (4.1.169)

Chi è il mercante qui, e chi l'ebreo?
Chi è il terrorista qui, e chi è l'arabo?
Chi predica qui, e chi ascolta il Suo silenzio?

Chi sta col gregge qui, e chi coi lupi?
Chi sta coi lupi qui, e chi con volpi?
Chi vive di sogni qui, e chi di incubi?

Quale cosa è vera più d'un bimbo ferito?
Cosa ci porta il vento del deserto, quali pianti?
Fedele alle parole, a voci, a dubbi,

Tu scarti pelle, sangue, voci interne.
Gridi: *Un coltello mi strazia la schiena,*
Chi domanda la sua libbra di carne?

The hungry, the thirsty, the stranger

I am hungry, for sanity in my life.
You are thirsty, for water that is real.
We are strangers, for that old deceit
a natural family divided by a ghost.

Still in the womb, we fought, brother,
for rank and when we came out
we tricked our father into his blessing.
We carried wood since then for our pyre.

Tired wanderers, now we need a truce,
a space, a meal, a drink and one voice,
lest we keep on killing more lives that
Abraham gave. Peace onto you. Peace to me.

Let's yield up images that can't be real
but attune to hunger, thirst and our terror
in the perennial walking over neither mine
nor yours, but our true Mother, Nature's

hundred faces of desert-white sands.

2013

Gods' obituary

The news of the demise of the gods
is, to say the least, exaggerated.
Jupiter for one, is alive and well,
banging on in the shape of a priapic

swan within Yeats' Leda, while Juno
– you'll find her in many shopping malls
loaded with noisy bags and small children,
and the shadow of a Thurber husband.

As to Allah, thank you, I rest my case
while Jehovah, isn't he ever ready to split
in three equal (or is it consubstantial)
persons? Even Lucretius had to dedicate

the much alive *De Rerum* to Venus,
to try and prove that gods were dead.
Listen to him, the gods are to die
when the last of us self-destructs.

2013

Seeking asylum

(After Haydn)

And God said: *Let there be man.*
And a man is
now on a trough, now on a crest.

And God said: *Let there be flight.*
And a seabird's shadow
shelters man and his plank of shipwreck.

And man cried: *Can you see land?*
And, giant wings resting on a warmer current,
the bird soars, drops, its shadow ebbing on his only bond:
No, I can't.

And God said: *Let there be wind.*
And wind blows and grows
and draws foam from the east-south-east
and the seabird buffets circles tries to shade man
until his death.

And after a day of Creation,
God turns in to a well-deserved rest.

2013

Bureaucrazies

I
Returns

This is to advise I shall be arriving on December Twenty Fifth (25).
Would you please try and arrange for a manger,
a warm-breathed donkey and a small ripe cow,
a Mother, a Putative Father, and three Kings
ready to bring myrrh at a time to be mutually agreed.
I shall be arranging for the accommodation of one Angel
and for the manifestation of one Nova in the Southern Sky.
Should there be any disagreement as to My Nature,
there shall be established an Administrative Tribunal
in Nicea, sometime from now. You are of course aware
that I know what was, is and will be, therefore there is no need
for any Agenda papers, other than a ream of clean papyrus
to be inscribed with the words: Here Shall Be Told.

And nothing more for now, except a warm note of thanks
for all the trouble you will be causing Me
to prove a simple point. That is, as you were informed
in previous correspondence, to make good one (1)
one only, Original Defect in the manufacture.
There is no guarantee, of course, that after what must happen,
the slight defect of collective guilt for all taxpayers
will be completely clean of Evil Lust and Inclinations
or that the womb of all future mothers will carry
true fear and faith. It may be useful if a basin or a font of water
is kept at the ready for use. I hope this is clear.

Let me also add that any Apparition or Trembling of the Earth
or Light-in-the-Sky is beyond claiming through insurance
if causing distress, broken glass or exsanguination.

I am sure that the benefit of this initiative will extend much beyond this place and the current expenditure from the common purse will accrue benefits beyond all your time.
Yours Faithfully etc etc.

II
Retrained

By now force-retired, a middle-aged journo,
       I wear an Arafat demi-beard
       mowed low-white with a small sharp scythe
       and have enrolled in a community college
       for a two-year course of navigation
       on nuclear submarines.

By now fully certified (only two hundred hours
       behind the electron periscope) I trudge
       from wharf to alien dry-dock
       responding
       to calls for skipper for commodore
       of any air-navy strike force.

By now retrained I will
       re-train again for first mate
       to a pastry-cook in the marzipan ship-shop.
       A diplomatic diploma will be added
       to the wall
       of the man-cave that's now
       my silent space proper.

III

Chairing

She sailed into the story as if in a space
of sea and wind. The languages were strong,
the voices averring *you are tu sei egli is*.
The declarations of mutual respect,
multiples of the same word repeated
all over the large hall through loudspeakers.
Alien the words to nobody, translations would sear
words into minds, receptive as flowers
of black asphalt or bread dough
of a crown of blue crust. The Chairwoman
made all sit down with a gesture. Clean scrubbed
like an Icelandic maiden she spoke Mandarin
to the left, Arabic to the centre in the hall.
Two other officials of the governing body
spoke black dialects, one hidden in priestly pink
tightly arsed trousers. Never
a word in anger. The consultations
started when the creative word was given
the green light and the Russian Samoyed Italian
mutually unintelligible representatives
started speaking. The voices were playing
with the echoes and the Hungarian-Chinese
transcriber would cup a hand to her ear.
Large portraits of Captain Nemo, Ulysses
transported under the belly of a mutton,
adorned the United Nations,
two small truth-lamps at each side.
The first proposition was to resolve
a matter of principle on boundaries between
wind and sea. Vento e mare. ветер и море.
The last never came as the Secretary of State
exercised the best power of veto.
The Chair? She vanished as print in an aging scroll.

2014

In memoriam

He died like a man. He died.
He died like a hero. He died.
He died like a wimp. He died.

Good men, bad men. We die.
Like raging fools, asking why,
shedding our last tear, we die.

Blinded by the light of god,
finding nothing but a fraud,
we leave nothing but gnawed

bones for just a little more
of the time allotted to our
atoms to stick, and no roar

of rage or wave of inner peace
will in any way affect the peace,
the universe's tumultuous peace.

Stars continue. One is born.
Universes are created. One is born.
Infinity begets infinity. One is born.

No time left. No one to mourn.

2014

Immaginario

I

Ecco dunque, fratello, inventiamo
al di sopra del Buon Dio
un dio buono: l'azzardo è abolito dalla vita.
Uguale ogni destino, non c'è alto, basso, bello, disforme,
nulla chiama al raffronto perché la somma bontà
non permette dìspari vite
nè che scatti dall'arco
la speranza, già egemone freccia
ai figli del Buon Dio.

Inventiamolo, quindi, un dio bonario
che non spacci offerta di meglio
magari nel dopo della vita,
che non smerci il sù e il giù
e nemmeno il meno ed il più verde,
nè porga all'uccellino l'ansia
dell'uccello rapace d'artiglio
che strappa il rosso tessuto e vivo.

All'ombra dei campanili senza suono
non c'è più sprone a chiedere suffragio,
perché il dio buono non ci danna.
Non ci danna all'usura della suprema astuzia
o al carisma dei paramenti
o al superbo gesto del principe.

E, di sicuro, alza fratello ora il tuo sguardo
a questo nuovo sole:
tu lo intendi, anch'esso è buono,
perché non odia se stesso e non s'immola
a nutrire filiali, cannibali pianeti
della sua stessa rovina.

Imaginary

I

Now then, brother, let's invent
above the Good Lord
a lord who is good: all peril is abolished from life.
All destinies are equal, there's no high, low, beautiful, deformed,
there's no call for comparison because the supreme good
allows no disparate lives
nor any slippage from the arc
of hope, now the hegemonic arrow
of the Good Lord's children.

Let's invent him, then, a good-hearted lord
who doesn't put off better prospects
maybe until after life,
who doesn't go around selling up and down
and not even more or less green,
nor plant fear in the nestling
of the bird of prey with the talon
that tears apart the red and living tissue.

In the shadow of soundless belltowers
there's no incentive to beg alms,
because the good lord does not damn us.
He does not damn us to the usury of supreme cunning
or to the charisma of cope and surplice
or to the proud deportment of princes.

And, for sure, brother lift your eyes
to this new sun:
you understand, it too is good,
because it doesn't hate itself, will not immolate itself
to nurture child cannibal planets
out of its own ruin.

E all'universo non è richiesto competere
con altri universi, paralleli o convergenti,
e quindi esso nè si espande nè assottiglia
verso il non-tempo nel non-spazio:
rimane calmo, fermo.

E, come l'universo, fermo il sole,
e, come fermo l'uccellino,
tu rimani, fermo, a rappresentare
—a nessuno—la fissità costante
impressa in tutti dal dio buono.

And the universe is not required to compete
with other universes, parallel or convergent,
and so it neither expands nor thins away
towards non-time in non-space:
it remains calm, still.

And, like the universe, the sun is still,
and, as the nestling is still,
you too remain, still, to represent
—to no-one—the constant fixity
Impressed upon all by the good lord.

II

Ma ecco, quindi, un dio incattivito,
magari dalla noia d'essere solo,
del non avere conforto
nella gioia d'un Verbo
e che, come un maestro
direttore d'una orchestra di fuoco,
col gesto capriccioso dell'esperto
fa sorgere
qui una roteante galàssia
che verte al suicidio,
qui pianeti interstellari
e sopra l'onnipotente voragine
che anela a divorare il creato.
Sul nulla e nel nessuno
si poggia il potere dello iddìo
che non sa più essere che iniquo.

Il sottrarre e l'aggiungere
(che per l'essere terreno
rappresenta la morte nella vita)
è per quel dio come l'aratro
nel vasto campo da arare,
come nel volo dei rosei pappagalli
l'ultimo chicco di frumento,
come il monatto per il ricco appestato,
come lo sterminio d'una foresta
e d'una folla falciata
dai colpi di mitraglia del tiranno.

Non ha sosta e non ha scranno
questo dio-maestro, astioso
perché il suo gesto ha l'urgenza
della colata di luminosa eterea lava.
E non si ferma.

II

But, well, look, a god turned nasty,
probably out of boredom from being alone,
from having no comfort
in the joy of a Word
and who, like some fiery
maestro orchestral conductor,
with the whimsical gesture of the expert
brings rising
here a rotating galaxy
involving suicide,
here interstellar planets
and above the omnipotent whirlpool
gasping to devour creation.
On nothing and on no-one
rests the power of a god
who no longer knows how to be anything but evil.

Subtraction and addition
(which for earthly beings
represents death in life)
is for this god like the plough
in the vast field awaiting ploughing,
like in the flight of rosy parrots
the last kernel of wheat,
like the corpse-bearer for the rich man stricken with the plague,
like the extermination of a forest
and of a multitude scythed
by shots from the tyrant's machine-gun.

He knows no rest and knows no throne
this maestro-god, ruthless
because his gesture has the urgency
of the flow of luminous ethereal lava.
And he does not stop.

Trascende gli astri
s'intruppa s'intrufola
in ogni minimo spazio
di là di qua del tempo
e non tralascia di torturare
ogni confusa mente.

He transcends the stars
he joins on he slips in
into every last minimal space
that side this side of time
and does not leave off torturing
every last confused mind.

III

Immaginiamo ora l'ultimo secondo dell'ultimo minuto
e, contenuto in questo, l'ultimo pensiero: vedo il Tuo volto
scolpito non nel marmo ma nel flusso d'un'acqua sorgiva,
o nell'istante di questa leggera nebbia che chiude quest'inverno,

e in questa nuvola rosa che annuncia la lunghissima sera.
Nell'Idea fulminante che chiude ogni altra idea: Tu sei.
Non guidi e non chiedi guida, nè sei più lontano di me da me,
nè più elusivo della mente dell' altro e, come questo giorno

si perde non più in uno nuovo, so che Tu non puoi essere cattivo
o buono, ma Tu solo contieni l'idea che dà significato
a tutto: al sole e all'altre stelle e al parlamento degli uomini,
ai miei figli ed alle parvenze di cruda carne

che invade questo creato. Si, è l'amore che sfugge
ma è il reale. Ed è quello che più non penso ma sento,
e che in quest'ultimo secondo dell'ultimissimo minuto
lascio andare, perché il tempo d'amare è tutto ormai compiuto.

III

Now let us imagine the last second of the last minute
and, contained within this, the last thought: I see Your face
carved not in marble but in the stream of water from a spring,
or in the instant of this light mist that closes in this winter,

and in this roseate cloud announcing the longest of evenings.
In the thundering Idea enclosing every other idea: You are.
You do not guide and you ask for no guide, you are no further from me than I am,
nor more elusive from the mind than others are and, as this day

is no more lost than a new day will be, I know that You cannot be evil
or good, but You alone contain the idea that gives meaning
to everything: to the sun and the other stars and to the parliament of men,
to my children and to the appearances of crude flesh

invading this creation. Yes, it is love that slips away
but it is what is real. And it is that I no longer think but feel,
and in this last second of the very last minute
I am letting it go, because by this time the time to love is finished.

2012

Saints

Saints, one per calendar day.
Great Saints for Great Nations
Small saints for a nugatory.

All feed names to the newly born
but the psychopomps alone
safely guide souls
to the place of the dead.

Healers of village plagues,
intercessors, advocates,
disrupters of flows of lava
and of enemy armies,
saints must however
stay well behind the throne.

In earshot of the choir
of prayers, they are forbidden
to partake of any incense
wafting from the golden bowl
of the worshippers
singing down below.

*Question: Does the singing of the saints
change with the singers' song?*

Together with the thaumaturges
all saints are elected
to their elevated post
by tiny groups of men.
Patrons of a village,
a battleship or a nation,

saints stay in their office
until they are sacked
for lack of ammunition,
of rain or maybe too much.

While on the job they toil
for peace, safe driving
and, in the trenches, for killing
rather than being killed.

They share their sheltering
duties with angels,
both entrusted with our passage
through the earthly tour
gutted of too much worry.

Now, why do you suggest
that custodians—saints and angels—
might not work
always in the fullest accord?

I was told there is an explanation.
But I forgot what it is.
I beg your pardon.

*Question: Do our Angels and Saints
talk to foreign saints and angels?*

When the fiery flow is unstoppable
and the plague unstymiable,
the saint is carried out, on the street
in blue finery, gold and scarlet,
and, by acclamation, sacked.
It isn't clear what happens
in the heavens.
Maybe they migrate
across the paradisiacal

gardens in search of better luck.
After all, Baba K is reincarnation
of Lord B who moved up to be Saint Peter
and still migrates from one
into the other pontifex.

*Question: Is there an arrest of comprehension
between Catholic and Muslim heavens?*

Now that we have grown global,
saints, martyrs, even archangels,
elected by all religions,
freely travel, but still gravitate
not too near the centre
of the kingdom, not so distant
as to disallow our prayers
to be heard through intercession.

No, there is no arrest of understanding.
Proof is the ongoing experience
across all earthly regions
of healings, peace-makings, births of sane
children, of birds sustained by breezes,
wellsprings of laughter in *piazza* and in forest clearings,
of sunrises and sunsets,
of blessings imparted by the elderly departing
for lives well lived,
and tears of joy by those who persist in being.

Of course, the battle-side hospitals.
Of course the eating of the flesh.
With the blessings, part of a whole
that includes all saints.

2015

Runaway bride

The Bride has run away from the altar
leaving, scattered, fronds of honeysuckle.
Frozen old-man-marble the Vicar.
Frozen the Sistine Choir.
One by one, Cardinals, red-robins, freeze.
Bishops freeze under roof-scraping hats,
bell ringers dangle mid-air
at the bell ropes. Incunabula

and papyrus rolls, illuminated bibs,
ashes of burnt books freeze, epiphanies,
revolutions of celestial orbs
tin-truths of tinny trinities:
all prophecies accomplished,
the virgin Bride can now be gone
and let us be glad and rejoice.

2014

Lament

Son, the moment He began courting us,
had we been a little smarter we should
have run from the charm and the toadying,
the flattering portraits of ancestors

painted deep in caves at Lascaux:
'Go! Run! Better die than living as stock!'
But we did not run. Our fate was set:
billions of men still live off our flesh

and when poets poetize about us
isn't their hypocrisy so very gross?
'Milk, a gift. Skin, smooth as silk'
and then our flesh is reviled as 'meat.'

How many tears were wasted at the shock
when man, made in the image of God
The Abstinent, was unveiled as a fraud,
forever, till the cows come home,

a coward who milks out your mum, cowed.

2017

Sentinel

'What's in being animate: is the soul required
or can one live without,   like an autómatón?'

The query came when,   sunning at Sydney Heads,
we saw upon us Talos,   the giant once of bronze,
old sentinel of Europa,   who now runs the rounds
faster, stronger than ever   along the Australian borders.

Re-cast in solid crystal,   to shield our gold, from
plundering hordes that try and pierce our border
ignoring that it is etched   in ink on the seawater.

Nearly identical in looks,   Talos and I, it was he
made in my image, not I in his. Nor was there
 an Eve: a man was sole ancestor in the lineage
but, one selfish bastard, kept all reserves of soul
deep in the bowels of a banker's stronghold.
Yet, inside whirring gears and transistors, some soul
was hatching for this semi-rational question:

'A rabbi made a rabbit golem, a pope a parson's
nose, Frankenstein a monster that was horny:
Creator-man, why can't this robot have a soul,
a heart beating a little beyond the reason of border?'

2015

Antiche bombe e il Coronavirus

La più piccola era senza scarpe,
un vestitino già bianco e tirava
tirava la vacca che, di solito
tranquilla, sembrava oggi distratta
dai gatti del mezzadro. La sorella
più grande, calmly led the cow,
full of milk, eyes slow as her pace

e c'era un altra ragazza, sguardo lento
curioso. Seguiva con un catino
di zinco ed un pesante sgabello su
per i gradoni di santa maria
apparente, fermandosi poi quando
qualcuna altra ragazza scendeva
da qualche appartamento al terzo
o quarto piano, con una scodella
verde di coccio e nel pugno chiuso,
poche monetine. Lo scambio era
rapido e spesso silenzioso.

Il latte saliva così nelle cucine.
Quasi tutte piccole, erano, e buie,
e bastava l'olfatto a far sapere
quale di capra e quale fosse latte di vaccina.
Di notte c'era puntuale, il cambio di scena.
Fra gli aereoplani dei cosiddetti alleati,

li cannun' ch'shparavan' da terra.
E c'erano i proiettili traccianti ca
lasciavano linee'e fummo e lucevano
verde e puzzavano differente dalle bombe.

Ancient bombs and the Coronavirus

The smallest had no shoes,
a faded little dress and she was pulling
pulling the cow which, usually
calm, today seemed perplexed
by the smallholder's cats. The older
sister calmamente guidava la vacca,
di latte piena, occhi lenti come il passo

and there was another girl, with a slow
and curious look. She followed with a zinc
basin and a heavy stool
up the steps of Santa Maria
Apparente, stopping when
a few other girls came down
from some apartments on the third
or fourth floor, with a green
earthenware soup bowl and in a closed fist,
a few coins. The exchange was
quick and often silent.

This was how milk went up into the kitchens.
Almost all little, they were, and dark,
and a sniff was all it took to know
which was goat's milk and which cow's.
Every night it happened precisely, the change of scene.
Between the aeroplanes of the so-called allies,

the cannon firing from the ground.
And there was the trace fire of shells
leaving lines and smoke and glowed
green and had a different stink from the bombs.

E di certo diverso dall'inodore Coronavirus.
Sono passata ottantanni. Come si spiega il ricordo
così vivo che appare scompare
al rumore ai giochi di luce della televisione.

And certainly different from the odourless Coronavirus.
Eighty years have passed. How do you explain a memory
so alive it appears disappears
at the noise at the play of flickering light on the television.

2020

Mandela

Lo incontrai, una foto sullo specchio
dal barbiere Cimmino nel centro di Chicago.
Camice bianco, volto grigio e vecchio,
mi aveva sogguardato di lato e di riflesso
e non mi disse *Come glieli taglio?*
Gli avevo chiesto io, distratto, chi fosse
il negro nel ritaglio, con la riga, fiero.
Mi indicò un piccolo graffito, *Invictus*,
e due altre foto ma sul muro
– Frederick Douglass, abolizionista
e liberto, Daisy Bates, dietro a una finestra
infranta, nata libera ma ancora segregata.
E disse infine il nome, che suonava italiano,
mandàla, e mi colpì perché fra i buddisti
è l'universo e per Freud invece è l'arcano
simbolo dell' unità di ogni essere umano.

Lo incontrai di nuovo, una sera,
pure in una foto ma coi capelli bianchi.
Era a Napoli, esposto nella via Forcella
nel tabernacolo della Madonna Nera,
ma col graffito: LIBERATO MANDELA!
Proprio a Forcella c'era ancora
guerra, ma non fra bianchi e neri
ma fra la camorra—il male—e la gente.
Era una forma di segregazione,
si dice ancora, tenere un popolo intero
ostaggio di quell'altro oltraggio
alla sovranità di chi liberamente
si associa in una Costituzione,
nell'unità di ogni essere umano.
C'era chi lottava lì e ancora lotta,

Mandela

I met him, a photo on the mirror
at Cimmino the barber's in central Chicago.
White coat, grey face and old,
he had eyed me furtively sidelong and reflected
and he did not say to me *How do you want it cut?*
I had asked him, unthinkingly, who was
the black man in the clipping, with the parting, proud.
He pointed out some lettering, *Invictus*,
and two other photos though these were on the wall
– Frederick Douglass, abolitionist
and freedman, Daisy Bates, behind a shattered
window, born free but still segregated.
And finally he said the name, which sounded Italian,
mandàla, and it struck me because among Buddhists
that is the universe and for Freud by contrast it is the arcane
symbol of the unity of every human being.

I met him again, one evening,
in a photo once again but with white hair.
It was in Naples, displayed in Via Forcella
in the tabernacle of the Black Madonna,
but with the legend: MANDELA FREED!
Right there in Forcella there was still
war, but not between whites and blacks
but between the camorra—evil—and the people.
It was a form of segregation,
they still say today, keeping an entire people
hostage to that other outrage
to the sovereignty of those who freely
associate in a Constitution,
in the unity of every human being.
There were those who fought there and fight still,

anche a nome dei princìpi di Mandela
per esempio, Roberto Saviano.

Infine lo incontrai di persona
dopo il Nobel, alla TV australiana
e mi ero preparato all'intervista
non come se andassi incontro a un santo
da venerare o, Dio ci scampi, a un dio.
Mi ridussi alla mia essenza minore,
a quella che vereconda dice *ti rispetto*
ma non ti adora e solo ti vede
come un uomo raro, il cui confronto
non è Gesù nè Gandhi, ma Mandela:

raro, come tu che leggi sei rara,
dall'alfa all'òmega, come lui granello
di nulla nel dapprima e nel dopo,
ma pure una scintilla di luce
così forte da impartire a te stessa
il dono più grande, che è l'amare
luminosamente la tua, nel rispetto
dell' interna unità di ogni altra vita.

even in the name of Mandela's principles
for instance, Roberto Saviano.

At last I met him in person
after the Nobel, on Australian TV
and I had prepared for the interview
not as though I was drawing near a saint
to be venerated or, God forbid, a god.
I reduced myself to my own inconsequential essence,
that which meekly says *I respect you*
but does not worship you and sees you only
as a rare man, whose likeness
is not Jesus nor Gandhi, but Mandela:

rare, as you who are reading this are rare,
from alpha to omega, like him a granule
of nothingness in the before and in the after,
but still a glimmer of light
so strong it imparts to itself
the greatest of gifts, which is luminously
to love your own, with respect
for the internal unity of every other life.

2013

Disimparare

Ci vogliono tanti libri da disleggere,
dipinti da disvedere, musica da dissuonare,
maestri da disascoltare—infine per disimparare.

Ci vogliono illusioni da smantellare,
credenze da discredere, emozioni da smontare,
affetti da disconnetere—per togliersi quel peso.

E se allo stesso tempo smussiamo
i sensi—vista udito sapore olfatto e tatto—
troviamo, finalmente sopita, la tempesta

del vivere come un essere senziente.
Un'altro inizio, vuoto di emozioni,
vuoto di stagioni. Ora sei libero

di disvedere dissuonare disudire dispiangere.
Quanto a me, provo ma non posso cancellare
l'odore della paura, il sibilo d'una bomba

che cade, il cranio schiacciato d'un fanciullo.
Ed ora lo stesso grido che viene
dai nipoti di noi allora bambini

sotto lo stesso sole, ma in Siria, in Gaza.
È la mia ribellione contro il disimparare.
Ma che ne beneficierà? Non tu

creatura nata d'esuli nel campo di concentramento,
nè tu, bimbo che ti porti il sogno
entro il filo spinato del tuo tempo del sogno.

Unlearning

It takes many books to unread,
images to unview, music to unsing,
teachers to unlisten, finally to unlearn.

It takes illusions to dismantle,
beliefs to disbelieve, sorrows to disable,
lovers to disconnect, finally to disburden.

And if you also unsharpen the senses
of sight, hearing, taste and touch and smell
you find the storm suddenly abated

of a lifetime as a sentient being.
Another beginning, void of feeling,
void of seasons. You are able

to unview unplay unlisten unwhimper.
As for me, I try but can't unlearn
the smell of fear, the whistle of a bomb

falling, the crushed brain of a child.
And now the same scream from
the grandchildren of those children

under the same sun, in Syria, in Gaza.
It is my rebellion against unlearning.
But who is to benefit? Not you

child born of exiles in the exile camp,
nor you, child carrying the dream
in the barbed wire of your dreamtime.

2013

Ginger

I don't remember summers
other than summers of war,
three, four, six counting two invasions
of the ginger rogers' allied forces.

Was there time to go swimming?
Was it in oil-blackened rubble,
oranges, turds, near aircraft
carriers, ginger-grey and green?
And if I tried the on-the-back
position, did I see the pale sky
through a net of barrage balloons?

Turn again, now wrinkly child,
time to wake. Leave the sweet
anguish, the wet dreams of blood.
Abandon those ginger summers of fear.

2014

III

Illogical digressions from serious present-day matters

(An inverted abecedarian)

Zany silly quirky cuckoo
Year in year out flies through.
Xmas in Sydney is his ideal
Winters far, warmth nearer.

Vagrant, chooses nests by night,
Ousts native parents too weak to fight.
Steals space by stealth, pushes chicks out
Reducing them to the nest outer margins.

Qualm-absent cuckoos never quaver:
Panic, screams, tremblings are no saviour.
On the rocks below, fallen, in pain until their last breath
No indigenous chick could escape death.

Morning afternoon nights
Lebensraum at top of gums
Koo-koo the *Hymn to Joy*
Hiding all that was the ploy.

CODA
Habeas corpus at The Hague:
Generals Judges Experts, a plague.

Fabulists then take over,
Extermination eugenicists,
Decimation doctors.

FINALE
Coo-coo Koo-koo,
Born again:
Aryan.

2020

The question

There was once a monkey who asked *who am I?*
The answer was not one that would satisfy.
Some time later he climbed down from her tree,
looked at the sky and asked *pray, who am me?*

If the four words seem grammatically incorrect,
they posited a question that took time to reflect.
Later still, not the monkey but her descendants
reset the question—*what is our why, our essence?*

It was the moment He had waited for. He cancels
the Lease, calls the Quick Eviction Angels
and both he and she had to leave the trees

and grassy lawns and tepid sea-breezes.
Yet, the questions kept on rising to the sky
and I for one still ask *who the heck am I?*

2016

The art of self-deprecation

It begins when still in the womb
overhearing that in the ultrasound
you look a bit like a dachshund.

Light-blinded in the birth-room
but not deaf: *nose is a bit overgrown.*
Years later mother makes you known

to all as *a bright eyed lad but plain.*
Wisdom not there already to protect,
the confidence-shaking quips you collect,

lettres de cachet into your own Chateau d'If,
continues, unabated, as you master the art
of twisting all you hear—eyes that dart

away, discreet coughs, innocent pauses—
into braids of self-defeat. Until you meet
the other half, almost a virgin, and you greet

your shared infirmities of the heart.
You sit on the mossy tree trunk on the sand
here on your beach and the unplanned

journey begins through each others' truths.
You make amends. You talk and kiss
until a golden twilight rises

from your faces up to the sun
who will not colour the sea tonight
wine-purple, but true black and true white.

2013

... And foundering is sweet in such a sea

Giacomo Leopardi, 'L'Infinito' (1819)

My Mum taught me to rhyme and count syllables
Cá-ro Báb-*bo*, natural as the heart's thump'n whoosh
or the dawn and dusk throb of pigeons on our roof.
At primary school an unforgettable teacher
made us memorize poetry which, he said,
is like storing energy that is in words
powered to fly up, beyond time and logic.

E il naufragar m'è dolce in questo mare,
and foundering is sweet in such a sea,
is still first on recall. It has taken me to havens
of light when in pain or fear, and now as ever
helps me to infinite streams of stillness,
to gardens that have a voice, or silent hills
to look out from, onto our calmest valley.

2016

You asked me

You asked me
to bring one
thing
of mine
and one poem
wrapped around it.

The fact is
the entire universe
is a thing
of my mind.
No part
can be separated
from it.

Yet, as my desire
is to please
you, fellow
verse spinners,
I ask your creative minds
to project
on this Lone Cave
Library's wall

the Pure Form
of a poem of mine
still to be written,
wrapped in the
still to come shadow
of the
thinnest ever
hypothetical,

Pure Fact
folio.

2019

Áccent accént

Join me in a planned undertaking,
that is, a project to project our desire
to increase our joys and to desire increase
of the fairest ideals and to produce
produce that nourishes soul and body
for the poor and hungry. To do this
we shall not need to rebel with arms
but become rebels in the heart,
not to outwardly protest against protest
in the street but to record good
deeds and build a record of peaceful
impact of what impacts most on minds,
to inspire men to defect from defect,
object to the cult of the object,
subject themselves to the subject
of living in the present, and present
what is most relevant to the peace,
because in your own content you find
content that is the first attribute
to attríbute, in the desert that is life,
the dessert of tranquility of the heart.
Invalid in the heart no more. Invalid
is all that you have discarded.

2015

Evolution's true crown

In the beginning were oats, millet and wheat,
windswept waves of free-born grains
in the savannahs of Africa's green plains.

One day, an ape scouting for his luck
gave up on trees, migrating with wife
and children for a grain-foraging new life.

Worn fossil molars, alas, tell the sad story.
Energy was misspent on chewing raw grain
rather than on growing a still puny brain.

History's turnaround came with a discovery.
Grains could be ground between stone and briar
wetted by rain, cooked by lightning fire,

and bread was! soft in the centre,
with a festive aroma, crunchy crown
easy on the molars, round oblong white-brown.

Digestion time shortened, the brain grew
and soon the ape would call herself Man.
The rest is well-known. Brains that plan

took Marco Polo to Asia and to the garlic,
Amerìgo to the American tomato,
Galileo to the oil so loved by Plato,

Saint Thomas to the flowering oregàno,
and with these ingredients on a disc of dough,
well salted, soft hearted, reddish glow,

pizza was! evolution's highest crown.

2014

Middle ages

There was a hawk that flew each day
to the gloved hand of a hawker.
There was a hawker who flew off
the handle when his hawk didn't fly
to his raised gloved hand.

There were a handle and gloved hawker
who flew high into the air to meet
half-way like trains in a medieval knight
and there were a hawk, a handle and a hawker

that stalled to ground sadly woebegone.

2013

What is a cow?

What is a cow?
Nothing more than two consonants
and a vowel,
cutting light on this sheet
in the shape of a c, an o, a double u,
casting a shadow
on grassland
or in the cage
where her udder's teats
are tethered
to my
or your
cash cow account.

2018

Danny Lovecraft

Why did the canny mind of Danny
suggest to poor me that I wrote a triolet
A poetic form so silly that's really uncanny
Why did the canny mind of Danny
Made me go through such distress. Yet
why do the canny mind of Danny
still I do prize well above all the rest?

2020

The country of *hmm* and *like*

Our great land of fillers like *hmm* and *like*,
of perpetual laughing, tonsils & caries in sight,
of lame songs sung swallowing the 'mike'
by decrepitating adolescents
who fake orgasmic delights.

2014

Funneling the nation

unsmiling guests arrive at the scene it is just after nine pm
stiffer they won't leave one act later at the latitude of four pm
who was in can stay as servant of whomever came
later this simply was established our nation
this simply was established any nation
you knew didn't you but of course
it makes for the historians
a task too easy much
better arrange for
many the ruse
of freedom's
funnel
per
co
la
t
i
n
g

t
o

all

2013

Fence sitters

'coloro/che visser sanza'nfamie e sanza lodo'
Dante, *Inferno*, III 36-36

    Fence Sitters   *Fence Sitters*
I love fence sitters [who are] true to peace   I hate fence sitters [who are] untrue to peace
[as to] war [equidistant from] law [as to] crime   [as to war [as distant from] law [as to] crime.
Dexterity [is] gauche. Sinesterness [may be] right.   Dexterity [is not] gauche. Sinisterness [won't be] righ
Cas[ting] a shadow over the truth   Cast[ing] no shadow over the lie
of a [midnight] moon in the sunlight.   of a [midnight] sun in moonlight.

[But] fence sitters [require more   [When] fence sitters [want less hate]
than love] require the dark wild forces   they reject the luminous forces
that make the skies rotate from right to left   that stop the skies rotate from left to right
and [when not observed] from left to right.   and [when observed] from left to theft,
upside down, until all [views] are a-blend[ed]   head upturned, until all [views] are suspended
[with what were] swishes and zigzags   [with what will be] christmas wishes
[be]yond with[in] the fence sitters' minds.   [be]yond with[out] the fence sitters' minds.

I love them in [the] world now coming   I hate them in [the] world now gone
where [all ideas are a-blended]   where [all ideas are separated]
Good [cute] bad [acute] obtuse [moral]   Good [cute] bad [acute] obtuse [moral]
ambiguised supremised lethalfellated   ambiguised supremised lethalfellated
mighty sitters [right and] left brain   mighty sitters [right and] left brain
anastomised [now] scream   anastomised [now] scream
cream [with me]: Hurray yarruH!   cream [with me]: Hurray yarruH!

Asymmetries

To Dario Fo

I

Yes, she will not put out his rages.
No, he won't interrupt her tears.
In a couple's asymmetrical warfare,
whose is the vulnerable system?

II

As Moon can't match
Sun at routine gravity games—
naked blue, eyes painted—Earth
squares up to both silence and roar
of fire, one mask of biblical reeds
on her northern hemisphere,
one red, obscene mouth painted
just above her cathartic forest
of pubic hair.

III

Priorities:
Exoplanets in Proxima Centauri?
Pink ice-rings who run around Uranus?
Syrian kids slowly dying of cold and hunger?

IV

Arcane more
than even space-time,
words, huàyú, wörter, λόγια, слова,
linger on, replete with false insights
such as   An. Eternal.   Life.

V

But right now, the Poetic Word
is the most unreliable
written as I am doing,
upended,
like a duck
who swishes
in this pond, underwater,
to mate with his harem
of salacious
biblical reed knots.

2020

Space semiotics

'Exoplanets orbiting Proxima Centauri!'
'Pink ice-rings around the planet Uranus!'

Go on, Man, promise you will also find
fellow clever beings swimming in latent
ponds of infinitely teeming space-time.

Go on, throw Arabic-Zenith and Latin-Umbra
at the nothingness of the universe above.
But know it won't be long before someone,

up there, grasps that mankind's tools of trade,
Words Parole Verba Wörter Λόγια, Слова,
are only a Biblical ruse to be *Logos* as God.

Maybe we won't remain so irrelevant to Nature
that anything remotely redolent of meaning
lingers to the end, unseen, in the teeming

void of a universal semiotic pond. Maybe
we will not be disrespected as a joke
by a god who now suspends the gleaming

Borealis and Australis Corona constellations
in the most luminous regions of the sky,
but upends the dark Corona Virus inside us.

2020

To make tea

To make tea you need,
Hot water
Leaves of Chinese camellia grown in Ceylon,
by the youngest kids and oldest grandmothers,
near chamomile flowers
to temper
theobromine effects
upon the shakers.
A pinkie that curls
in harmony with the cup whorls
and round slices of cucumber
in the sandwiches.
Try a glass teapot.
It is near invisible
so document the ceremony with a photo,
high res, b&w, contrasted.

2016

Nested riddles

Thirty pilgrims search for the author inside.¹
Two pilgrims then meet Voltaire and De Sade
on the trek to the small compost site.²
One pilgrim looks for a father,
one for a son—they eventually gather.³
From the city of woe to that of sky
everyman moves without asking why.⁴

Burdened by one book,⁵ we amble,
stumble. From the city of woe
to that of the sky, woman
and man walk talk walk
without asking where or why.

---

1 Who turned a Knight and his squire,
a Parson, a Nun, a Pardoner, and twentyfive
other characters, into scribes?
Had he known about the flying saucer,
would he have also chosen a Martian
to ghost-write a book for him,
the incomparable Geoffrey Chaucer?
(*The Canterbury Tales*, XIV century)

2 As Pierre and young Jean walk to Compostela,
they meet The Inquisitor, The Virgin and the Devil.
School girls recite heresies then scream 'anathema'.
Two blind men, miraculouly restored to sight
cannot understand what they see, cruel fate
or walk unaided in the film by Luis Buñuel.
(*La voi lactée*, 1969)

3 A book of enigmas and puzzles
that for centuries will keep critics
perplexed as to what JJ truly means.
To censors it was obscene
but students in generations to come
go straight the dirty bits in the tome.
(James Joyce, *Ulysses*, 1914-1922)

4 Christian is troubled by his sin.
Evangelist tells Christiana to leave him.
Obstinate and Pliable are a bore.
Let's leave them.
John Bunyan, *The Pilgrim's Progress from This World to That Which Is to Come; Delivered under the Similitude of a Dream* (1678)

5 *The Bible*

No need to look for history's troubles or divine puzzles over promised[6]
real-estate
bubbles. The instant man began to wander
away up down east west yonder,
the inherited fortune of staying put,
was misspent, went kaputt.

On this note, having pretty riddled,
being old and temporarily crippled,
I am ready for rest. Mme Sphinx:[7]
What did you say about the walk'n sticks?

2014

---

[6] Promise of the Land.

[7] "What walks on four feet in the morning, two in the afternoon and three at night?" Oedipus: "Man: as an infant, he crawls on all fours; as an adult, he walks on two legs and; in old age, he walks on three, a 'walking' stick."

Misquoting Shakespeare

To Mark O'Connor

Quote me, son, but earn that right.
He was sitting on the bed-edge, waiting for
me to wake. I did, surprised to see him
here of all places. He did not smile or say

'morning. On the night stand was
a conversion from English to English,
labor of love by Mark, the poet of
many sweet voices. The goal, simply,

to commit himself, his person, to let
people like me earn the right to hear
and quote. *Am I on the way?* I cried

afraid. Shrewdly vexed, He cried:
You still are one of many who rob
sans taste, from me, sans eyes.

2015

New Year's Eve litany of fears

Just joking

As I was running away from ghosts of times past
I saw new demons blocking the escape into a tomorrow
When the existence of evil powers would evaporate
At the rise of a dawn of reason. Then, unexpected,
A platoon of pitch black cockroaches, vanguard
To legions of spiders, long-legged, fattened
By untold numbers of flies, bees, wasps, even bats,
each no less worthy of living than me, who anxiety
alone made into this blob of green fears. And beyond
spiders I saw snakes, heights, needles, rejection,
cocktail parties, even dreams of public speaking,
long past exams, failures, open and enclosed spaces.

The silly games played at New Year's Eve!

2016

Miti sinistri

Radiazione cosmica di fondo.
Radio-onde terrestri.
Nello sfondo, sovrano, il mito.

Oh sismica sinistrità del sasso Sisifeo che si fracassa a valle!
Ah densa intensità d'incensi alla Messa in Remissione dei Peccati!
Assettati figlia mia e udiscimi.
Il Cielo sibila,
ronza e il radiotelescopio
cileno d'Atacàma
sul Cerro Toco
ancora risuona
degli antichi miti

Oh radiazione comica di fondo, spettacolo di luci che riempe l'Etere!
Ah l'inganno che parole siano qui in Terra scelte per riflettere!
L'ingannevole calma
governa,
l'eleganza
di vaporosi vuoti
s'adagia soffice
sulla nebulosa d'Orione
e quel remoto nome
rimbalza
cosmica radiazione
nella nostra mente.

Oh l'artificio della sorpresa scelta fra ogni possibile espressione!
Ah la bonomia seletta per se stessa da Selene!
Ma se la Luna ghigna
è una falsa benigna.
Se il Sole va alla morte
questa è la sorte
di ogni costellazione

Universal logic

Cosmic Microwave Background Radiation.
Earth's Radio waves.
Further in the background, sovereign, myth.

Oh the sisterly sinisterness of Cinderella's sisters.
Ah the frankly fraught frankincense of the Mass for Deadly Sins.
Sit down my son and listen.
The Universe whistles,
whirrs and in Atacama's
radio-telescope
on Chile's Cerro Toco
it also screeches
menacing myths.

Oh the very faintly comic sound-and-light show that fills the Ether.
Ah the deception that words are selected on Earth for their meaning.
Disturbing calm
is sovereign
as chicness is
when nothingness sheets
softly fall
on Orion Nebula
and their sound
rebounds
off the amphitheatre
of the highest
Earthly crater.

Oh the surprise artfully selected among the range of expressions.
Ah the good humour selected by Selene for her face.
The Moon leers
never stands still,
the Sun goes downhill.
and with them all myths.

ogni nome
ogni mito astrale.

Prova quanto ti pare, figlia, pensa finchè t'esplode la mente
finchè declini e appassisci tutta, senilmente,
la sinistrità dei miti
che s'ispirano al cielo
è il nocciolo stesso
d'ogni cosa che verte
nella nostra mente
ed ecco qui a ***
perché tutto
sembra sinistro
così assai sinistro.

*** Inserisci il nome della tua località.

Try as you will, son, try till you burst your mind
till you ebb and fade into old age's atrophic grind,
the sinisterness
of sky-inspired myth
is the pith of life
also here, in ***
it's sinister
so very sinister.

***Insert name of your locality.

2013

IV

A lesson

A tree exists as a seedling.
It grows. It breeds.
Self-changes or dies
just like this park's giant Moreton Bay Fig.
Long-time hide-out and food,
playground to possums and birds
today it had to be felled
by noisy municipal contractors.
Tonight, sawdust sadly
enshrouds the ground in place of the shadow.

Were it not for the curiosity of its roots
wouldn't it have been better
to grow just to a sapling?
The roots instead wanted to burrow
and writhe and learn more,
even to form strange alliances
all the way to distant parts of their world.

But then one day
the seedling's genetic urging to probe
was stymied by an ever-rising heat,
the one that we of our species alone know
comes from the nuclear core of the Globe.
Was it there and then that the roots
decided to stop their manic research?

The fact is the Moreton Bay tree now
is dead and we don't know why and I
for one am truly afraid of inquiring.

2017

Free-fall

Sometime in the past here grew an Oak.
Fed by sun and rain and being well grounded,
it spread out crowns of leaf and root,
only boundary being its imperial shadow.

Bold alliances with wind and gravity
let the smooth acorn and yellow leaf
fall so the Oak fed on itself while it created
colonies of fungi-perfumed new life.

But one autumn, at dawn, a dread commotion:
We can't find ground!—branches and leaves cried
in freefall. Our planet had gone on its orbit

leaving behind Mother of Oaks, her myths,
even the lofty poetry she was known
to modulate in times of storm.

2021

Come Lui li volle

I suoni a caso d'un vento eterno in una eterna selva,
non potranno non causare la 'Pastorale' di Beethoven.
A Michele Campanella

Quando entrammo nella selva dell'eterno caso
per ascoltare gli alberi nei giorni di tempesta,
non offriva ghigno di morte, il cielo, ma armonia
di vento e pioggia fra le foglie e le fronde.

Fu allora che scoprimmo che alberi dal timbro
preciso di violini, violoncelli, clarinetti ed oboi,
con l'eterno inclinarsi ed inarcarsi
concertavano armonie di verità surreale.

Rami cadenti sulle cave rovine di tronchi
offrivano chiarità di contrappunti percussivi
e, assieme a trinità di picchi a caso picchianti,
tendevano alla singolarità d'un ultimo evento.

Solo in questa eterna foresta, dato tempo
per ogni possibile convergere del vero,
intuimmo che avremmo alla fine ascoltato
come vanno eseguiti, come Lui li volle,

il Gewitter, Sturm, Allegro ed attendendo
ancora più eòni ed eternità di tempo,
l'Hirtengesang, la canzone grata dei pastori.
La foresta potrà allora finire e così il tempo.

As He wanted

Given infinite time, random forest sound
would almost surely produce Beethoven's 'Pastoral' Symphony.
                              To Michele Campanella

While still in the forest of infinite chance
we listened to trees in the days of storm,
no frown of death from skies but harmony
of wind and rain through leaves and fronds.

We found tone-wood with the precise timbre
of violins, cellos, clarinets and oboes
that when trees bent, swayed and swung,
sang in concert with reeds, yielding to wind.

Branches falling on abandoned hollow trunks
provided counterpoint of percussive clarity
as did, by pecking, trinities of woodpeckers,
in concert towards one last event: a singularity.

Only in the forest of infinite chance, given time
for all possible assemblies of truths,
we knew we would eventually hear
as it should be played, as He wanted,

the deaf master's Gewitter, Sturm, Allegro
and, if we waited a few eons longer,
the Hirtengesang, the shepherds' thanksgiving song.
The forest of infinite chance may then close.

2013

Parola e Logos

A John Bryson

Giù per il fiume dall'Università delle Montagne,
girando a destra pei Prati del Dolore
ed a sinistra al Parcheggio di Thredbo,
troverai una antica signora.
Si agita e lamenta con pause pensate:
'Rivalutate narrative, storie, canzoni e forme di danza.
Incoraggiate il dialogo fra chi chiede e chi afferma,
cioè quelli che chiedono sapendo la risposta
e quelli che nitriscono
come giumente di notte
al trotto sopra tombe scolpite nella pietra di fiume
e piangono "non lo sappiamo." '
C'è storia scritta nel fiume
che non cambia come l'acqua passa
e rinnova cibo per le trote.
Lo chiamarono Logos perché non c'era Parola a quel tempo.
Non suono.
Per riprenderlo occorre la clarità della sorgente
nutrita di neve montana,
di incontri che creano nuovi strati di sapere.
Su per il fiume. Giù per il fiume.
Parola rincorre Logos e Logos si ferma
immobile come parola affettuosa,
mentre il professore di fisica spiega
il testo dove Parola è in fuga,
Mito è scacciato e Logos è fermo
qui alla fine del Thredbo River.
Tu ti fermi ed ascolti la vecchia signora
se è ancora disposta a incoraggiare
questa antichissima danza.

Word and Logos

To John Bryson

Down the river from the University of the Mountains,
turning right to the Meadows of Sorrow
and left to the Turnstyle of Thredbo Creek Parking,
you'll find an old lady.
She agitates and moans with strategic pauses:
'Re-evaluate narratives, stories, songs and forms of dance.
Foster dialogue between those who ask and those who tell,
those who ask knowing the reply and those who neigh
like night horses tramping over the graves
sculpted in the river stones
and whose cry is "we don't know." '
There is history written in the river
that doesn't change as the water goes
and renews feed for the trout.
They hate-love the fly-fisher,
their story is ancient like the first sound.
They (not the trout) called him Logos
as there was no Word then.
No sound.
To retrieve it now the clarity is needed
of the spring fed by mountain snow,
of the encounters that enrich layers of meaning.

Up the river. Down the river:
Word chases Logos and Logos stops immobile
as a term of endearment,
while the physics professor explains
a text where Word is chased,
Myth eschewed and Logos stops
here at the end of Thredbo River.
You too stop and listen to the old lady.
If she is still prepared to foster this ancient dance.   *2014*

The bees

Selections from Virgil's Georgics (IV)

And, now, hear about the gods' airborne gift of honey to mankind,
the amazing drama of bees, their science, customs and wars:
so tiny so frail to our eyes, yet capable of immolation for a cause.
Times were when, free, bees hived in hollows of rotting trees.

Now, hives can be sold at the mall but their cells are still as of old:
stately for a long-living queen; cramped for expendable workers;
magic cells for liquid gold, joined through six identical corners
where Leonardo could have, but did not, draw The Vitruvian Bee.

First, hunt for a site not exposed to southerly busters
that push returning nectar-full bees away from the hive,
and safe from calves who stray from the pastures
and foul the bees' crystal-clear drink of dew.

Next, screen off goannas climbing trees not for flowers
but honeybees, said to clean fetid carrion from their mouthparts.
At all hours, citrus plants will perfume your beehive
As will Grevilleas, Magnolias and Myrtle flowers.

If you have a pond, scatter branches and round stones in it
as islands for bees to rest tired wings during nor'easters.
Last, while bees need space to land, to enter leave a mere slit
They can fortify against weather and foes

as winters harden and summers let molten honey slip.
After a long absence, as you reapproach your hive,
you may be puzzled not hearing the familiar buzz.
All gone! Despair when you arrive, as no Queen

or drone is left to continue the genetic line.
Calm down. Hear the method revealed by Virgil

On how a bullock's body may beget bees.
Warning: It is creepy, a first account, verbal,

from the most ancient kinsfolk of the Nile.
After choosing a room fit for the crime:
– four windows to let in all the ill-winds,
walls easy to wash of blood with lime –

bring in a bullock, his horns only still
a bulge, soft on his head. His breath,
through chained nostrils and mouth,
soon is a rattle as he is beaten, beaten

to a red pulp, through his unbroken hide.
The killers now leave him, having strewn leaves
of fresh thyme and rosemary over the body.
It will stay there, alone, uncovered, until

warm easterly winds again whip the waves,
meadows brighten up reborn with colours,
and swallows revive nests of mud under the eaves.
Meanwhile, as the corpse warms in the new season

and ferments, the most arcane creature heaves,
without feet at first, but soon growing wings
and trying the air until it can fly out,
multiplying like rain from nimbostratus

clouds, or arrows from the twanging bows:
a miraculous, reborn swarm of your bees.

2023

A wailing sonnet

Another window is ripped open
in the quivering canvas of this theatre-set.
Fire-trail. Wallabies. Ant hills. Native
wild blood calling for loud conflict.

Only half-caste, no gift for words,
yet he said—*this is the best time of life!*
If he could not now run for his stick,
on the fire trail he still was the wisest.

What layers of past did he carry?
Would he choose to be so gently killed?
Many men envy he had this freedom.

Free of the queer idea we need to let out
opinions, no matter how tedious,
he remains at the ready—still unworded.

2014

House hunting

Two lorikeets climbing down the flue
of the main fireplace
study the dark depths and take notes.

All the best branches of the trees
captured by stronger birds,
there is no space for a new family
to start a household in the full sun.

Many leave. Some commit suicide.
But those with hope-green tail feathers
and vivacious eyes take a roundabout route
to throw off pursuit by predators also hungry

for space and bird meat. The white peak
of bricks just cleaned-out
by the tiny chimney sweeper
seems like a Strait of Gibraltar

inviting crossing. But fear takes over
from the patient climbing. Unwillingly
the wings take life and start
fluttering beyond the control
of lorikeet reason. They shriek.

They awake the household that assumes
the cold fireplace is haunted by rats.
                A fire is started.

2011

Lyrebird

Here are three families of lyrebird
cornered in remnants of tropical forest
near our homes,
you wouldn't know them
as they mostly hide
under a priestly black garment
and, when they sing,
it's not their own lyrics but those of others:
chatter of lorikeets
lament of chain-saws
even screams and laughter.
Here is a lyrebird whose specialty is to bark
when I call out for my dog to please come back.
Lyrebirds own no one language. They borrow
from whomever is closest to their very fine ear.

Myself? Owned by two, or is it three, tongues
and an infinity of inner callings and sounds,
I move unaware of which is the voice
and how it feels to be in possession,
firmly, of what I might call my truest language.

2013

Wallaby tracks

She cried, 'You have to see this!' and I rushed out the kitchen door onto the beach freshly washed by rain not arrested by a fresh arrival of seaweed whose colour was like the rocky beach with white spots of worn out oyster shell and we stopped because there was a long light stripe darker than the sand ochre and wasn't straight but zig-zagged a bit and there were regular marks on each side that she had understood were the large feet and mighty tail of a wallaby and maybe it was the one we saw the night before so unaware of our dog so unaware of the danger that was us but led by one only thought and that was cabbages, tomatoes and Italian lettuce in our new veggie patch up in the garden and the wallaby could not know it was ours because all land there was his or hers to roam and forage and we were mortified of the wallaby-proof fence and we went back into the kitchen with few words to say but she had taken three photographs to remember and then I rolled out some paper and wrote this

2016

The birth of myths

October is ripening the vines,
chrysanthemums also are in season,
birth, death in the air, fruit, flowers,
humble honeybees, boat people.

Aware of fate, keen-eyed dolphins
ritually encircle boats, now coffins.
Unaware of myth, a she-whale
suckles twin orphans. A new tale?

Beasts don't need to atone. And us?
We flay our bodies, wear hairshirts,
spurn rebirth, devoutly wish to have
been left unmade in the womb of Earth.

Il nascere dei miti

È ottobre. Matura l'uva nei vigneti,
i crisantemi sono di stagione,
e attorno nati e morti, frutti, fiori,
e barche cariche di disperazione.

Ligi al destino, sfilano delfini
solenni attorno agli annegati.
E, ignara del mito, la balena
offre postremo latte a due piccini.

Alle bestie non si addice penitenza.
Noi umani ci sferziamo, sfoggiamo
cilici, sognando d'esser stati lasciati
increati nel grembo della Terra.

2016

Tribunal: Hearing at dawn

The hearing starts at dawn.
Seven of the blackest crows
sit in session on the low

branch of the spotted gum,
to make a ruling on today's weather.
The case opens with the Defence.

She argues for a non-guilty day,
full of the joys of early spring
while the Crown blusters that the day

is at once the best and worst:
generous at night of strain

and of the day's sun. Sundry
dissent on the upper branches
are quickly quenched. The carpet

python, the goanna are on the scent.
What the birds in the jury conclude
we find nowhere recorded.

2011

Closure

December, forty-two degrees.
Our beach empty but for the army.
Blue soldier crabs
and Her Pickiness
the egret who feeds on them,

Peering out of pinholes in wet sand
more than you can count
are tiny articulated eyes on stalks,
eyes that see and, in a flash,
withdraw to safety in the sand.

Is it the blue soldier crab-way
to stem waterfalls of inner tears
at becoming aware of the outside,
assuming blue crabs are empowered to cry?

Maybe closure is pulling heads
deeper into sand but closing the past doesn't guarantee
that we can move along
only that we declare an episode obsolete.
Yes, the past has ways to stick around.
Remember, it is called history.
History, unlike dampness on a hot windy day,
is never a thing of the past.

2015

Non sequitur

When he disclosed her father had spoken
to him in stern tones saw he did not.

A glint in his eyes, a former spoilt child
not afraid of things done in haste.

A future darkly read on cards. Serious
talk without the expected undertones.

But respect despite beauty from the top down
makes the talk tone change. And then

the arrival is signalled by warm-up sounds
in the still tuning orchestra of the morning

so proper to the reddish shafts of sunlight
that pierce clouds or maybe that just stand

quiet, waiting for the sails on the left horizon
to come forward with seagulls astride.

We get up early in these quiet mornings.
Avalon is ahead. Scotland Island on the right,

the sea lane lit by no sound other than
the still tuning orchestra of the mind.

Numbers of birds some alone like the grey
egret or the sea eagles of Woody Point.

Some gregarious biters like the loud white
parrots crested yellow like dinosaurs,

all concerting as nature tunes its tools,
even the silent microbats that roost

in the boom covers in their thousands.
We go up top and find them even there

and won't know if they are playful or not.
Take a breath. The day may go quietly longer

than expected. Only a few lines down
I should reach the five hundred words

not about music nor poetry, who is that
who reads that nonsense. thou certainly not.

Those pronouns neither fly nor evoke egrets,
the weird punctuation. the pretentious stop

and go, hinting at sense, some sense at all.
Repeat with me: repeat with me. Repeat.

Those archaic pronouns neither fly nor
evoke egrets and sweet islands in a Pacific pond.

rather they remind of the caiman who
caught a frog and the frog said let's make a deal

lodge me and I shall dislodge all refuse
from your pharynx causing streptococcal throat.

Her father was unmoved.

2021

Pittwater

T'interni, mare, a costruire un lago
d'insenature dai nomi recenti.
Gentilmente offri lo sciabordìo
della tua onda e ti appai e ti spai

dai fusti sempreverdi, che frenano
la furia del sole dalle cicale
indistinte dalla corteccia grigia
e viola. Scorre amichevolmente

la cappa verde, di baia in baia,
da collina a collinetta, di rado
scoscesa, al raro camminatore
assai dolce. Tu permettesti a pochi

pacifico approdo e in questo lago
sembri amico fidato a chi trasporti.
Ma tu non ti ribelli o ti opponi
agli incendi boschivi. Ti rifugi

in segrete alleanze con le armade
di squali-martello ticks ragni serpi,
ai fruscìi sinistri che urgono 'vai via.'
Poi, visibilmente, offri i colori

dei pesci-farfalla e giorni tenui
di vento e parchi d'onda. Si crede
all'inganno e si rimane a sfidarti
su barche il cui andare trascende

Pittwater

Insinuate, that's what you do, my sea,
to build this lake, these bays just named.
Gently you offer with swaying swooshes
to marry and quickly unmarry the evergreen

trees, that act as a brake against the fury
of the sun and shelter the cicadas
indistinct from the bark violet
and grey. Congenial, the verdant canopy

streams from bay to bay,
from hill to mount, rarely
steep, to the rare hiker sweet.
Yet only seldom you did consent

to uncontrasted anchorage in this lake
you pretend is trustable and a friend
to those you ferry. But you do not rebel
against or oppose the bushfires. You take

refuge in secret alliances with the armadas
of hammer-head sharks, ticks, spiders, snakes,
with the sinister rustle
that urges 'go away.' Then you parade

the colours of the butterfly-fish
and days tenuous of wind and shy
of wave. We fall for your deceit
and remain to challenge you

i confini di etichetta marina
e in villaggi bersaglio del tuo moto
e rovina. Eppure, ti ho eletto
a luogo del mio spirito, furtivo

forse, con malpiazzato orgoglio.

on boats that transcend all boundaries
of marine etiquette and in settlements
that are targets to your motion
and ruin. And yet, Pittwater, I did elect

you as the place of my spirit, furtive
maybe, and with ill-placed pride.

2012

Le colline dormono ormai

Le colline dormono ormai.
Incoronano d'ombre questa baia.
Solo vestigio del giorno passato
è l'umore che resta,
pesante, viola ancora per poco,
sul chiudersi delle colline
a ponente. Il pescatorello
si perde negli anelli
di onde concentriche
figliate dalla lenza.
Muta di sempre e nulla
questa acqua quasi
si chiude d'ombra.

The hills are now asleep

The hills are now asleep
crowning the bay with shadows.
Only vestige of the day now gone,
a violet mood lingers heavy
for a while more
on the setting sky. The fisherboy
is lost in the family of rings
the line impartially spawns
in concentric waves
over this closed sea
crowned with colourless shadows.

2012

When sails are born

It's when sails are born
out of the womb of sail bags.
They start flapping against the lazy
wind of the in-between seasons,
it's when she won't stay the course
and hold the swaying,
that the opaque warming
morning stirs curses
under one's visible breath
at the mast that won't stay put
at the creaking of the arching
timbers at the voice
that inside calls for the truth
of a stiff storm
or the becalmed day-after-day
darkness of the Sea of the Sargassi.

It's the midway that is unnerving
when unbowed by the flights
of the mind, dried.

2012

Spare a thought

He was after all a Lord,
the Pitt that won this water,
and a Tory. There is no recorded struggle.
Two reams of paper filed
at Westminster, an Act to follow,
eons of ritual meals
signed into prehistories of shells.
The spearing, the long wakes
under questioning stars
were now over alien land
alien river
under alien rain.

Those who were indivisible
from grass trees
were left with demons and dreams
and uteri that spurt
whiter beings for alien kings to disown.

Yet, stratified with ashes, pebbles, flint,
the easy to gather shells
are not the only reminder
as Junior Pitt and the line of mediocre kings and queens
were no match for the demons and dreams
who walk the shores in the deep of night
white as memes that recur and mess
with our uneasy sleep.

2017

Like Argos

There lay the hound Argos, full of vermin; yet even now, when he marked Odysseus standing near, he wagged his tail and dropped both his ears, but nearer to his master he had no longer strength to move.

Homer, *Odyssey*, 17.209

Do you dream now
can you still dream daylight?

We had come back to the bays
from a long sail north
where we had seen
amazing birds and whales,
told tall stories,
broken canvas
and lived the thrill of gales.

When we retrieved Papagena
from her carer
she was another.
True, unlike Argos
no cow and mule dung heap
no fleas, her blanket was clean
but like the king sailor's dog
at our newly found voices
her ears mildly rose
her tail wagged
and soon she nobly retreated
into worlds of long sleeps
rolled into her own
blind dog corner.

You had been the whitehottest noise
in Woody Point's spotted gums and casuarina
and no wallaby could be faster,
but, no killer,
you would stop at loudly accented
brief chases and never did you
maim or bite
although only flight
did save
the spiteful cormorant.

Do you remember what sight was?
What a bird was, Papagena?
Do you dream now
can you still dream daylight?

2016

Funeral for a wallaby

To Edwina and Patrizia

A small dark form against the sun
in the morning water. All is calm
when the neighbour
cries from her side of the beach
Is it our turtle? Softly the pressure of tide
brings it a little closer and the clear sea,
in between the rays of the rising sun, bares
the long tail, a lump of seaweed
with a small head.
A dead wallaby. And *I have grandchildren
just coming.* Sight. Smell. Fear
of death. Emotions curbed within a kind smile.
Then my wife comes to help
as I stand, watching. A team!

They find a long eucalyptus branch fallen
on the sand, light enough to steer.
Two women engage the poor corpse.
Two women pull it on a driftwood plank
then walk carrying the hearse
in a plain march.

The big honey-coloured dog,
the small white and black,
follow in eager procession
not knowing if this is lunch
or sharing of sorrow.

The only man there, I wonder
'Birth, death—why don't women
take charge of the whole Universe,
dell'universo intero?'

2014

Deep-wading

I made it all up
and yet at low ebb
all came to be true.

Seashells, stony pods,
lean grasses of the sea,
crab hideways
in ghostly dunes,
keen octopus eyeing
rays' pectoral fins,
pretences of peace
between wave and wave,
mock and true chases,
lies, trenches, veneers.

I must invent,
fantasise two truths,
make it all up,
build the story-lie
no matter if under
the new kingtide
it is war or peace.

Where I live, blows
always a wet-dry wind.

2014

House lifting

Between springs and neaps,
a one-handed man,
pushes like an Australian Sisyphus,
titanic steel beams
over roller contraptions,
mocking and pushing
through muddy and rocky beach.

It was here since he can remember,
upheld by a cast of oysters
encrusting sawlogged timber walls
the colour of a waning sun.

Was the little house self-born
like tadpoles do in stagnant water
darkly fostering their own body-plan?
They miss a tail but spark
with inner electric charges.

It is an eternity since, one-handed,
the hero started, alone on this house.
It rises and falls with each moon,
beached alive since time immemorial.
He will lift it up to be higher
than the highest king tide
Old man Sisyphus prepares
a feast for the eyes
of ravens, parrots and magpies,
and lost loot for a sea unfriendly
that is not the colour of wine.

2013

Tide of tides

It will be June, month of high tides
in this god-forsaking corner of the Pacific Ocean.

Well past our estuary, past the marshes
and the worms drilling into pylons,
past the blue soldier-crabs
immersed in their writing on the sands,
she will be force-feeding these broken bays.

Self-important, that queen of tides
will be higher than ever seen at the anxious gauge
and we shall watch but won't rush to any other corner,
watch as she pauses at the fireplaces
to try perhaps one last smoke,
while mounting floor, windows, and the horizon line.

Listen: the silence will be unbroken.
She will leisurely rest over the wrinkled roof
of the beach-house.

Inhale: has the smell of the sea changed?
Listen more: has the sound changed of the new winter?
Is the sun rotating with piercing sights of flames?
No, and it's no use distracting your attention
or keeping it fixed on the idea of your own demise.

Will these paintings float?
Will these chairs remain anchored
to the convivial table?
And this ream of paper, will it be toy to waves
and feed to plankton?

Will I still be here or, from some place above,
evergreen, see the sea again slowly withdraw
under the shadows of the leafy pediment,
each day faintly more generous to the shore?
For a long second there had been this dying expectation
based on reading news from other islands
at other corners of this alien Ocean,
fallen to the long hand of man's outgrowth.

But when it comes, you find it is flush with all imagination
and less scary. It's a fact
natural as this seepage from broken vessels,
brown blood on the hands,
the failing equilibrium
or the pose each day more bent.

Earth is ageing. These bays age,
this old beach saw the ritual feasting.
These verses rhyme-less and are scanty of clear sense.
But the oscillations of the moon, like of taste,
sweep away bad and good
but hand back any overdue payment
in the fullness
of astronomical time.

2012

V

Come di sera d'estate

Come di sera d'estate
dalla casa intessuta di mare e vissuta
di rampicanti abbrancati a decenni
di fumo (il fumatore di pipa)
si guarda al cielo affollato

costellazioni invisibili
a quelli nella città vicina,
più lontana
della distanza in ore e miglia

come di sera a fine estate
si guarda dentro e ci si parla
senza più parole
con la sorpresa ferma di chi vede stelle
e nebule dove già neon
e, chiuse in forme antiche
'motel,' 'petrol pump,' 'pizzabar'

è di sera che avverti l'estate
che chiude e torna Orione
a ricordarci l'autunno e le morte stagioni
e la presente
evviva!
        non le scorie d'un passato recente.

Rifuggire,
l'unica strada rimasta
porta qui proprio qui dentro
dove non ha nessuno a sovvertire
a chiedere di essere troncato a portar acqua
dove fuoco si chiede

As on a summer's evening

As on a summer's evening
from the house interleaved with the sea and alive
with creepers shepherded for decades
in smoke (from the pipe smoker)
one looks to the crowded sky

invisible constellations
to those in the city nearby,
further away
than distance in hours and miles

as on an evening at the end of summer
one looks within and talks to oneself
with no words left
with the still surprise of one who sees stars
and nebulae where once was neon
and, closed in the old forms,
'motel,' 'petrol pump,' 'pizzabar'

it is in the evening you notice the summer
is closing and Orion is returning
to remind us of autumn and the dead seasons
and that which present
is alive, hooray!
                        not the scum of a recent past.

Retreat,
the only path left
leads here precisely here within
where there is no-one undermining
asking to be let off carrying water
where fire is what is needed

e fuoco dove solo si cerca refrigerio
da chi comprende troppo e non sa nulla
più nulla della casa intessuta di mare e di stoviglie incrinate

dove risuonano, unvoiced,
monosillabici 'yep' 'cool'
là dove si erano poi chieste
due magari anche tre parole che dicessero
'vediamo' 'esploriamo.'

Forse c'è più nella vita
del rancore.
Perché particolarmente nelle sere d'estate
l'autunno ormai alle porte e suona Orione
l'arpa del cacciatore d'anime, non c'è più
da aspettare. Il treno è pronto a ripartire

come ogni sera è pronto a fine d'ogni estate.

and fire where all anyone is looking for is coolness
from those who understand too much and know nothing
nothing more of the house interleaved with the sea and of cracked kitchenware

where are heard, unvoiced,
monosyllables 'yep' 'cool'
where what had been asked for
were two even three words that said
'we'll see' 'let's explore it.'

Perhaps there is more in life
than spite.
Because particularly in summer evenings
autumn already at the door and Orion playing
the harp of the hunter of souls, there is nothing more
to expect. The train is ready to depart

as every evening it is ready at the end of every summer.

2002

Carpe Diem a Balmain

(omaggio ad Orazio)

C'è modo migliore di dire ciò che provi,
che con vampe rubino sulle fossette evasive,
con l'ambiguo smeraldo delle ciglia?

Qui, sullo sgabello blu sul marciapiede.
Qui il labrador, ormeggiato ai fumi
del bus quattrocentoquarantaquattro

avverte a naso: *un macchiato un cappuccino*!
Guarda. Rilascia le tue salde braccia.
Lui ti parla, animato. Ma tu osserva: quei due altri

camminano cauti tenendoai teneri per mano.
Osserva come il tuo lui non segua il tuo sguardo
nè avverta la ormai svanita vampata.

Tu vedi invece come il mattino sia breve
in questo villaggio dentro questa nuova urbe.
Tu sai che il tepido sole si scava veloce la via,

oltre l'angolo di questo povero cafè di ricchi discinti
di questo mondo lontano. *Carpe diem quam
minimum credula postero.* Non posso dirti altro.

Carpe Diem in Balmain

(Homage to Horace)

How can you better say what you now feel
than with a ruby blush over evasive dimples
and one sly flutter of emerald eyelashes?

Here, you sit on blue bottle-crates,
close to him and to the paving dust.
Here the labrador, moored at the fumes

of the four four four bus, wags the tail
at the scent: *One macchiato. One cappuccino*!
Now look around. Let your arms go.

Let go listening to this boy's lively voice.
Look at those two people who slowly walk
tenderly holding hands that are mottled.

See how your man won't follow your gaze
nor is he aware of the vaporized blush.
It is you who knows morning is brief

in this crude village within this new
city. You know the lukewarm sun
runs its route faster around this corner,

beyond cafès full of young people,
chic in the poor ways of this rich place.
Long as it is the young wait for tomorrow

hold on to this moment, Leuconoe, hold on.
Do not chase future options, just hold on.
Carpe diem, quam minimum credula postero.

Don't presume there will be a tomorrow. *2013*

Elkington Park: The thriller

Unattended. He broods as the moon shadows
exposed the royal roots. Look around. No one
in sight. No light from the remote windows, the night
glows as wished by the owl and the prowling
bandicoot. Is the time now ripe to again
tempt fate? There is still one soundless warning
all may not be as quiet as it now appears
to the tired darting eye, the fearful ear, to the glove
that holds the poison. His own heart beat?

Tranquillity was the name given to the largest
of the Moreton Bay Figs, the main attraction
for miles to the squealing squadrons of clever
flying foxes. No one will ever know why
the noblest of these green palaces was abandoned.
It is these days only a provider of shrunken
figs to nervous day birds and rotting
mulch, soft to the feet of the runner
who slows under the decaying shadows.

2012

Homeless

Let me sleep as old dogs do
on a ragged blanket
as weary of sleeping
as of waking
to one more first light.

Let me stay
forgotten
threadbare
as these rags
kept as surety
for days of improbable cold.

Let my heart slow to one beat,
my arms to one gesture
my brain to one thought
but let it be one last conceit.

Let my hair fall
and the skin around my skull
shrink to filmy leather.

Let my flesh be food
for life with no eyes
no ears no feet no lungs.

Let winged beings
eat worms fed on my tendons
then discard me
within seeds of jacaranda
for new trees to grow
with my molecules
my atoms my nothing.

Let all life carry on
let it fill any void:
a white new blossom
a new cloud
the chick of an eagle
a cry of a newborn
a wave encircling a surfer
but not a child beggar
not a dull parliament of men
not a church of altered senses.

Towards the end of time
let the gods fulfil the promise
that all substance

nature lent us
draws towards one single point
where flesh reassembles.

But let me not endure
such resurrection
but remain asleep
no substance no dream
no more conscious thought.

Or please let me imagine
a 'me' not identical
but with zeal enough
to live a new existence:
with some knowledge
of what is to come
a 'me' with the skill
to push uphill
my large round stone.

Or allow me to float,
forever float as air does
above heavier gases
as oil does on water
as eternal words swim
on pages of wisdom
as rhyme prevails
over common-sense
as my body now hovers
over these fine marble steps
under the green
hedge-fund poster.

Let my eyes stay closed
but then
if possible
if the need becomes extreme
only then allow me
just a glance
at the shadows
of the two
by whom I was loved
during the flash of life
in my polite
cage of thought.

2015

Afternoon at the Art Gallery of NSW

The former wife reassesses
the lost familiarity with the rain.
'Did the President really say:
The world will still be the same?'

Sharp claws rake fine ochre gravel
that blend many-hued flower beds:
Aquamarines, reds, blues, yellows
clown up dour reptilian scales.

Raptured in the rare rain,
three water-dragons thrive
unafraid of humans. 'With good
food, evolution happens faster.'

'Matisse invented the future
so much more than…'
'Are you still alone?'
'I still am and so is my God.'

'Another decaf.' Whiffs
from a vanilla pod ease
the human fog: Immense,
over the gardens, glass

windows. 'So. Picasso?
Creator or chameleon?'
Final scamper to the cashier.
In due course all photos fade

in unimagined places
with round scissor holes.
A nod. Bus backlights flash:
Royal Botanic Gardens.

2020

En attendant Juliet

As time catches up
she goes faster
and, if she can't,
changes train

of thoughts,
slows them down,
watches
fellow passengers

watching
their watch,
won't step down
with them at the stop,

won't run away
but remains
steady and makes this
her very own

non-runaway train.

2016

Lost in translation

Black veiled woman
pushing a black pram.

Distant wrecks.

True to meaning
the graffiti means ساعدنى
but for you it may say:
Black veiled woman
pushing a black prawn

2012

Nosferatuner

Late summer. The pink lady is wilting
under the last ghost of the nor'easterlies.
The old Labrador howls on the jetty
at the absence of the she-consoler.
But after a long wait he is here.
Taller than the door, stoop,
fingers like braided snot
black suited under an illuminated
brain coat, a benign Nosferatu
with at the neck a tuning fork
whistling a forking tune.

2016

Utilities

Light switch, water tap, gas valve.
Gateways for the wages of my talent
to flow into the unknown
of shareholders' accounts
Elsewhere not rent:
        History as contrivance.

This is the world
Where you don't say 'workers.'
'Capital' is banned
From the politeness
of things that excise the past
From the present and traduce
Those words as feral
As voices of the unwashed:
        History as dead hand.

They discharge into mocking
Comment by the DJ
Whose mind is held up
By an elegant cravat
Crusading for liberty:
        History as nightmare.

2016

The new Pope

I am now slower, my own fast ways,
slow as quicksilver coming out of the absolute zero
slow as a python coiled in frozen motion
or as the newly elected Argentinian Pope
saintly proclaiming: go out, reach and teach, don't preach.
We are all the same, men of a certain age.
We have to display mature restraint
from passions, hate and love, anger and sloth.
Lead by example. Charity starts at a dinner table
loyal to Christ: timber planks, no cloth.

The new Pope must be sincere but, remember,
passions are all there seething in the depths
of decades of a life well or badly spent, with a cause
maybe beyond the gilt baroque hiding the cross
or, for me, other than seeing the end of this, or any, summer.

Il nuovo Papa

Sono ora più lento, nella mia rapida maniera,
lento come mercurio che esce dallo zero assoluto,
lento come silenziosa pantera pronta a scattare,
o come il neo-eletto Papa argentino
che santamente proclama: uscite, estendetevi e insegnate
ma non dal pulpito.
Siamo tutti lo stesso, uomini nell'età avanzata.
Dobbiamo mostrare ritegno maturo
dalle passioni, odio e amore, rabbia e ignavia.
Guida con l'esempio, caritas inizia ad una tavola
leale al Cristo, assi di legno, senza lini.

Il nuovo Papa è sincero ma, ricordati,
le passioni ribollono tutte lì nel profondo
di decenni di vita spesa bene o male, magari con un fine
che guardi oltre agli ori barocchi che tradiscono la croce
o, per me, oltre all'arrivare alla fine di questa o d'ogni estate.

2013

Rumour

The Priest
Had had an affair.
The chairs set
The bridegroom
Through the evening air
Anticipating rain
Thinks of that.

2020

Canberra Press Club

Ten prepared answers.
Here comes
the interrogation.
All answers drawn
by chance
regardless of question.
Hacks led
to post-prandial stupor,
the political dice
today also are drawn.

2020

Eye vision

Eye Vision surgery.
8 am and a windless morning.
7 elderly men won't eye each other
As they sit alongside clinically bare walls.

6 large women whose hairdos
brush the subdued white tones on the ceiling
also are still. All they produce is a motionless noise,
remote as their looking is remote.

Been waiting since dawn
will sit calmly here until dusk
maybe the tint of the walls
the white of the chairs will show
through them maybe they shall
vanishe
before the eye test
before the trans
                plant

They'll know the eyesight is restored when on
five coffee tables
4 plastic orchids wilt and
3 fashion glossies grind to
their vague shaking
    to a not too late end

2014

It catches up with us

It catches up with us, no matter what,
that tiredness of life when all is seen
to belong to the fulsome kin of *déjà vu*.
It may be in a sign, a sigh maybe,
at the daily repetition of gestures:
from the draining business of waking,
to reconciling the hoped sunny and new
with a score where all *is* repeats.

But—sudden—the chilling noise of dying.
Numbers roll on television screams.
Mask-less crowds sing hymns of praise

to the cull of Nature, when a new killer
is unleashed, uncaring, random, as all
that Stepmother Nature does best.

2021

Stockpiling

Stockpiling in anticipation of a famine:
we had all done *it* to survive *that* war.
It was flour, water, salt. Maybe four,
five books in near darkness to pore over.

What I can't recall stocking is toilet paper.
Maybe at the time it was a luxury item
well above our bottom line that included
fascist newspapers and, for the Dictator,

dreams of crude 40 to 60 grit sandpaper.

2020

Gifts: contemplations

The gift of cowardice

Muscles, tendons, ligaments, bone.
Wouldn't life be like lifeless stone
without nerves, our electrical soul?

Our science teacher was into rock-and-roll
of the necrodancer kind, you know,
electrocutions between muzzle and anus
to dance peacemongers out of the universe
or save them for nonsensical verse.

Soon our teacher grew dissatisfied
with teaching kids who would deride
his faith in life's electrical magic.
He left in a huff. No cries. Nil tragic.

Christ's atoms! Dionysus molecules!
Would life be still so cruel
if subverting all ground rules
rather than training children for war
with heroic smiles, with a coward's frown
we taught them how to back down?

Paler, he now preaches under neon
street lights outside a pub, The Treason.
From political dissidents were cries
when we run trials sticking needles in our eyes,
like Newton did, but found no dividing line
between nerve, nerves and spirits of wine.

The gift of delusion

In the Bass Strait, 1988

As if on a twenty cent coin,
equidistant to the rim
your small wheelhouse.

You grip, steer, look
at the labouring sails,
scan the night sky,
let your mind wonder.

Is there willpower
in this air motion?
Has the moon reflection
a will to transcend the horizon,
ride up the mast
and on the spreaders
flare up like a cross?

Do these flying fish
seek entry into heaven
and when they stall
who is willing them
back into the deep ?
Does that dolphin
lock eyes with you
so you won't fall asleep?

Grip. Steer. Deny
any proof of land,
stick to this fluid
idea of matter
because if this is all there is
it still is worthwhile.

The gift of self-deception

she walked in

mind stooped as from
the weight of birth-pains
as leaves of blue
cut out from the sky above
fell neatly into white precision
ready to receive them as words
if needed
even meanings into the windmill of
illogic elocution

she straightened a bit and continued:
black as black is to the overflow of prisons
shrill as shrill is to the trumpets of a revolution
sharp as sharp is to the blade of a word
that hints to a revenge for a future slight

she hinted perhaps to a revolution
that may also be a revelation
how to take the stoop out

perhaps she saw leaf-shaped cutouts
fly off the blue sheet of sky
blank markers for others to fill
with gouache colours
as the bedridden painter
did with his winning wand

she walked out

The gift of fire

You said they promise kids heaven.
I said we promise ours the war pension.
You said their after-life is a lie.
I said and so is our stated reason.

You said who brings back medieval terrors.
I said who owns warfare new horrors.
Their kids scream, index to the skies.
Ours dance, drugged to the eyes.

We all hide when we make children
otherwise who would dare to conceive
in a sunlight that nurtures terrors
and shows red darkened rivers.

We push back spilled gut with our hands.
They pull life out of ravines of prayer.
Whoever sends youth to die—god, nation—
may a common fire burn you all in damnation.

The gift of grace

if you sit here now in this stone garden
look on to the agave it has given birth to
this arch of triumph
built of seedlings and flowers
through which red-hot pokers cool the summer
and chattering magpie songs
enrich with unpredictable colour
the unkempt lawn
borders the high tide
graceful not always but in time
move your eyes to the inside
the part of creation that is inside you
the reality that has none outside
      to converse with
and look and quieten the stream
of discordant attentions
recall the noun
      grace
      the noun
that wasn't ever
properly explained to you
and still eludes
as in memory in calmness in circular flows
re-entry repetition reduction
from start to the end of times
      the world
      was created
      the world created Him
      Her and Them
and maybe even now
in this spring garden what we call
      Grace

2015/16

Un regalo gradito

(A G.M e F.C.)

Ci sono molti modi di vivere da amici.

C'è il dirsi grati per le mille cose
condivise in questa scintilla di vita:
un pianto, una cena,
forse uno scambiato sollievo,
una preghiera per quel morto.
E, complice, il sorriso
del sapersi mai remoti
anche se assenti.

C'è poi quel modo che pochi
sanno usare. Quello
di donare
del più vero sè stesso,
presentandolo magari
in un cuscino dipinto
all'antica maniera,
o in un servizio di piatti
sorprendentemente
vestiti di nero,
e magari anche in un dipinto,
quadretto-poemetto su tela,
che riflette mare e tronchi
sempreverdi
del luogo del mio spirito.

Come poi rinnovare
il grazie più vero
per tutti i doni
e per l'ultimo
semplicemente, unicamente,

A gift appreciated

(To G. M. and F. C.)

There are many ways to live as friends.

There is exchanging thanks for the thousand things
shared in this glimmer of life:
weeping, a dinner,
perhaps a shared relief,
a prayer for one who has died.
And, the accomplice, the smile
of knowing we are never remote
even if we are absent.

Then there is that way which few
know how to use. The one
of giving
the truest of oneself,
presenting it perhaps
on a pillow painted
in the ancient style,
or on a dinner service
surprisingly
dressed in black,
perhaps even in a painting,
a miniature-poemlet on canvas,
reflecting a sea and the trunks
of evergreen trees
of the place of my spirit.

How, then, to renew
the truest of thank-yous
for all of the gifts
and for the last one
simply, solely,

sinceramente sublime?

Ecco mi provo.

sincerely sublime?

Watch me try.

2012

One old woman

*Visiting Lis Kirkby at Morning Bay, NSW,
on her 95th birthday.*

Why doesn't she make you feel small, a mind like that,
bridge of memory across events, one only span, one person,
with little sign of the accruing seconds pushing at the exit door
– perhaps the voice breaking under the force of will
or the gait of the grand dame, now unassuming.

Erect as a bolt of energy, now from the smallest chair,
of course a fine one, upholstered with tapestry,
her small house confronts that other old woman, the sea,
not as even tempered or as tidy as she is recounting,
but as elegant as the essence of knowing is:

not of a past or a future that never is
but as a witness to myriad facts
so that the present is the only time for her.

And as she sits (a book on the fallacy of god worship
in the falling empire, in her reading corner,
a flute of Riesling she competently poured)
she not only recalls as the sea does but interprets events
whose turn it is to be the daily horrifier:
Daesh/IS
Trump who makes Putin appear as a sage,
the fellow ex-MP fallen to dementia.

Politicians, actors, doctors, maybe lovers,
grandchildren, ancestors from St Petersburg
names all neatly catalogued
ready for instantaneous recall
maybe once-only-seen professors eons ago
at the University of Toronto.

Well placed in this our species of mankind,
she soars above all,
'she' meaning her mind,
her unassuming greatness in this era
that for a magic moment didn't
reek for us of vacuum.

2016

If you publish a book

John publishes a book
that's met by deafening silence.
No reaction from the crowd
he sent it for reading.
Does it mean stop,
give up writing? He admits
there were worthy exceptions
– in Mado and Anna and Theo.
They were welcome.

John says, 'I will continue. But how to ignore
the sound of the borer self-doubt?'
And Anna: 'Why so bloody unsure?
Is it the travel between the two ways of speaking?'
'None is mine now,' says John
'Language and style,
verse and line vaporize
as each day runs faster its course.'
Mark joins in: 'Few
don't become obsolete
during their lifetime.'

But while you are still alive
with words that rush
and images that burn inside
and want out to ears and eyes
the dream of speaking
to any and all must continue.
Few could stop.

John asks: 'Were they the heroes?'

2012

At the gym

I expect that my inner safety switch will be
set off by these hell-hot, vile feasts of sound.

So I do the bike, do the dumbell squats,
dream ear-lids evolving at the speed of light.

To no avail. From walls, ceiling, TV screens,
the robots of rock work crowds into frenzies

of pubescent screamers and squealers
so invasive that any other thought

is stomped out. And I am left wondering
if rage is knowing or not knowing which

passions quake the adolescent billion
and if some will find our father, Bach's

St Matthew and St John's Passions.

2016

L'arte del conversare

A V.M.

La cena di ieri ci ha portato alla mente
che l'arte del conversare è nello stare attenti
a chi non parla. È nello spazio bianco,
nell'invito a riempirne i silenzi,

nel cercare lo sguardo più stanco,
il sorriso forzato e nel sincero chiedere
che ne pensi? ma senza raffreddare
i due amici che con alternanti

serietà e allegria annegano i centottanta
minuti della cena. Ed è anche nel rientrare
con loro dallo zio arciprete che abbandonò

Lipari alla fine dell'ottocento, e divagare
sulla perennità di tutto che sembra inattuale.
Quel mondo antico non era poi tutto lontano.

The art of conversation

To V. M.

Dinner yesterday reminded us
that the art of conversation is in staying attentive
to the one who is not speaking. It is in the blank space,
in the invitation to fill silences,

in seeking out the tired look,
the forced smile and sincerely asking
what do you think? but with no chill
for the two friends who alternating

seriousness and cheer drown the one hundred and eighty
minutes of dinner. And it is also in going back
with them to that old archpriest uncle who abandoned

Lipari at the end of the nineteenth century, and digressing
on the perpetuity of everything that seems outdated.
That world of long ago was not so far off, then.

2021

Cena domenicale

Il tranquillo ripetersi dei gesti.
Prendi i piatti.
Apparecchia la tavola.
Allinea posate e salviette
oliera e saliera.
Bolli l'acqua.
Butta la pasta, cibo
di rigore per gli stanchi.
Assapòra
i colori che risorgono al quieto
consumarsi della cena domenicale:
Durò per anni.
Poi nessuno più venne.
Non c'è più il dolore
della loro partenza.

Sunday dinner

The tranquil repetition of gestures.
Take out the dishes.
Set the table.
Align forks and napkins
salt and pepper.
The water boils.
Add pasta, staple fare
to the weary. Take pleasure
in skin tones
warming in the quiet
consuming of a Sunday dinner.
So it was for years.
Now no one ever comes.
There is no more the sorrow
at their departure.

2012

Patrizia at sixty

There are cool heads, even in the hottest of summers.
Take my wife, a woman whose faith is being kind.
At sixty she keeps, balanced in mid-air, her powerful willpower
fragmented in many colours, shapes, sudden changes of register
as an Alexander Calder mobile between opposing windows.

This season, much hotter than predicted, is a case in point
and I wonder how she can stay so steadily in tune with life.
Her age no constraint but a sense of today, magpies fly to her
unafraid of her dog, early in the morning, as she meditates away
the weight of time, her signature radiance new each new day.

2017

Idyll

There are two fine moulds in our mind.
One shapes space, the other steers time.
Senses can only pour into them shadows
And these then we mould as poetry, prose.

But the real light radiating in my mind,
From your luscious body, your bright mind
Keeps me surely folded in one, your mould.

2016

The day the internet died

The sick sulphur-crested white cockatoo,
black beak asymmetrically overgrown,
won't aim for now impossible figure eights,
on branches of our Himalayan cedar pine.

She just roosts where no flying foxes
dare hang, head down for an awake sleep.
She is a puzzle who visits, each day,
in the morning, early, shunned by her peers

but still with yellow well erect plumes
that now transmit danger with colours:
white-on-yellow flag that's death afloat

that lives on, a mourner at her own wake,
on death-watch yet on-track for treats.
Aftermath of funerals, civil while un-pious.

2021

Fidelio

As dogs do, my dog will not speak
but look intently on, look into my eyes
as I wait for words, and words never do come.

As dogs do, he reads all I think.
Even before I do, he knows my mood
and is quick to share with me his thought.

Yes, he is good at anything he does:
a scholar of grassy leaves, top encrypter
of scents, model of self-restraint

among the park pigeons, he smiles
to babies in strollers but not too near,
not too far to miss any of their milky essence.

I walk my life-way with him, exchange
reverences, and share all deepest emotions
with him, so wise, so unspoiled by speech.

2014

C'è un'ortensia in giardino

C'è un'ortensia in giardino, che ha fiorito fedele all'estate.
Si è offerta nei colori sia azzurro che pallido rosa
al capriccio di un'aggiunta di aceto o di bicarbonato.
C'è anche una vasta pianta di zucca che viaggia ed esplora
preceduta da fioroni imperiali giallo verde-nero,
e tante altre piante, tutte nutrite dal sangue, dalle ossa,
dalla polvere delle vite buie di tanti animali.
Ricordi l'asino e il contadino che lo frustava,
e spesso calava il bastone su quel dorso trasparente?
Ma ora l'asinello rivive la sua vita senza più dolore
nella baldoria d'estate. La pioggia diffonde i colori,
riflessi in nuovi rigagnoli. Perenne, il pero abbandona
qualche frutto. Passa il tempo e, in autunno, ortensie secche
nel vaso grigio verde-azzurro, parlano dell'esistenza con due pere.

There is an hortensia in the garden

There is an hortensia in the garden, flowering loyally to the summer.
It offers itself in colours, not only azure   but pale pink also
on the whim of added vinegar   or bicarbonate.
There is also a huge pumpkin plant   travelling and exploring
preceded by imperial clarion flowers   yellow green-black,
and so many other plants, all fed   on blood, on bones,
on the dust of the dark lives   of so many animals.
Do you remember the donkey and the farmer whipping him,
and how often the stick fell on that   transparent back?
But now that little donkey relives its life   with no more pain
in the merriment of summertime. The rain   diffuses colours,
reflected in new rivulets. Perennial,   the pear tree abandons
a few fruits. Time passes and, in autumn,   dry hortensias
in the grey blue-green vase, discuss existence with two pears.

2014

Aminya Place

Sunday walk in Riverview

Walking these streets you sense a void.
Things are missing and you wonder why.
The sign still says *Drive slowly, children at play*
but where are they? And this is where her mother,
Maria, lived, the house which her father
built, fifty years ago, opening up a street
for their then new friends from the ship.

They built with bricks the colour of honey
and, not like their ancestral landlords
with chalk-white columns and arches.
But where are those and where, wrapped
in nets against the scourge of possums,
the smuggled grapevine and the trees
not chosen for colour but their fruit?
You know each house now belongs
to middle-aged sons and daughters
who opted out of bloody balustrades and arches,
like most now do, for frameless glass.

As you go on with your Sunday walk,
you turn right at the Jesuits' Oval's bus stop,
and you aren't there either,
sitting in line, on the red fibre
school case that had been your sister's.

You know the void will reappear
tomorrow morning when you will
hurriedly pop pills out of their blister packs
and then at dinner time when the voided
blisters shall again face you, warning:
Monday Tuesday … Saturday Sunday,
each a withdrawal from your stock of time.

2016

Sisters

Today the walk went for longer.
The Labradors still pulled at the leash.
Another dog barked at their passing.
Then, as the first gate was closing
Bread still cooling on the windowsill
The colour of burnt flour turned,
To follow that single sparrow
Until the other girl raised
Her paler blue
Eyes to track
Imminent dark clouds.

2020

Mail stone

My leaf of gold, my truest, my routinely checked
mail, each day each hour, like water you take the shape
of the vessel you are poured in, like ice you are
stone, like a meadow you link two rivers that flow

one east one west. Yet, the one source is forever
for both, lost. The mountain that is behind
continues to be seat, passage, road, landscape,
finally to disappear. From all but the memory

where all converges and somersaults in, is then
archived, until the scions of years—forgotten
meanings—draw to a close. One stone after

another stone, the building that is mind
sheds floors. In the outside memory, remain
my kilobites, my routinely deleted

mail of these last days last hours,
like long-lasting tombstones.

Mail stone

Mia foglia d'oro, mia più vera, mia spesso scaricata email,
tu arrivi ogni giorno ogni ora.
Come acqua, prendi forma dal vaso che ti accoglie,
come ghiaccio sei pietra, come prato unisci due fiumi
che scorrono a est, a ovest. L'unica sorgente è per entrambi perduta.
Ma il monte tralasciato continua a essere
comune partenza e passaggio, strada e paesaggio.

Alla fine scompare.

Scompare da tutto ma non dalla memoria
dove tutto converge e si contorce e si archivia,
fino a che gli eredi del tempo—significati estinti—
portano alla sua chiusura.
Pietra dopo pietra,
quel palazzo che è la mente si sfronda dei suoi piani.

Ma nella memoria esterna, rimangono i kilobites,
le mie email regolarmente cestinate di questi
tardi anni, ultimi giorni, ultime ore,
quasi incancellabili pietre tombali

2014

And as I sit docile

And as I sit docile at a desk
in the middle of the main road
empty but for a cloud,
an image of authority
leans over my shoulder
and peers.

There is no paperwork
relevant to my position,
only a personal bill stamped *overdue,*
one or two beginnings
and a proof for a black and white.

He makes no comment
but I feel
I've overstayed my welcome.
It is time.
Every sense of being someone
evaporates
like a wave's crown of spray.

Are marine mists
all that remain of a lifetime of toil?
Or is there to be a repeat
where one minute adds again
to more and more
all remote, all now past,
all not the same?

But is it time?
I certainly won't ask
the Babylonian dice

as the gods dislike effrontery.
Rather, I shall cash in
the troopers' salary
even if I sense my duty has expired.

The cup is not full to the brim.
Leave time
for the overflow
and hope any addition
to my temporal lifetime
is a gentle one.

2011

VI

Trembling man

I am the trembling man.
I tremble therefore I am.
If the diagnosis is correct
will a Doppler effect
be my fuzzy main trait?

Slow but secure
I shall become a blur
a blear a mist a haze
and people will amaze
because, trembling man,
alone I know where I am.

2017

Hospital corners

Ah, those darn hospital bed corners!
A pock on barracks, sergeants and head-nurses,
on long edges, foot-edges and forty-five degree sheet angles:
> *pull one long edge*
> *tuck the hanging corner*
> *tight under the monster mattress.*

Repeat. Repeat.
Rage rage then and rant
about the darn, back-breaking,
imprisoning hospital corners.

2013

Ulysses

To Homer, Dante, Tennyson, Joyce and NASA

I will load the boat for my longest journey
and will have a noble crew, a crew of five,
recruited from one only source, who will arrive
each alone, each of them his own true king

and all sharing one single great name.
Each will have known all those who came before
but the first to arrive will pointedly ignore
the newcomers, won't shake hands, balking

each time he hears his own revered name
attributed to another, whose dress and tongue
he won't know—they look as from far-flung
places.   It's time now to explain. I invite

them to say where they came from,
who's their father and why are they king.
The first: 'I am Ithaca's true and only king,
the one who fought and won not on a horse

but on his feet. The blind story-teller,
not Laertes, was my true father. There
we shall leave my story.' The second's answer:
'I am the same man but my father was wicked,

he adopted and placed me as a flame in Hell,
maligning my wooden horse—a fraud, a bait.'
The third cries, ' … Come friends, 'tis not too late
to seek a newer world. Push off … let's go

to the untraveled world, whose margin fades
for ever and for ever when we move.'

The fourth is a thin man with thick glasses.
He throws cigarette ashes and thinks aloud:

'I am the true Ulysses. I waited so long
to tell my own story as it is the truest,
of me, me, me with hands in my pockets,
breaking asunder Logos and Word.'

The last, in truth, is a machine shiny as a star.
It whirred coming on board, now its voice
sounds as from sidereal distances, like Joyce:
'I am the space Ulysses, the probe

made to study Apollon, or Sun the median star.
And I have come on board to steer you all
—great poets like Dante or, like you skipper, small—
across the sidereal winds to the peace

of this voyage of very last release.'

2015

Quando

Quando all'appello d'un tranquillo pensiero
Si volge la mente a cose passate, quanti i vuoti
Fra le buone cose cercate mentre vecchie disgrazie
Riappaiono a sprecare il fuggente mio tempo.

Ma non inondo gli occhi, non uso versar lacrime
Per amici nella notte perpetua della morte,
Né per disgrazie d'amore da tempo archiviate,
O per tante speranze e progetti svaniti.

Allora posso angosciarmi per angosce trascorse,
E grevemente, di disgrazia in disgrazia, ripasso
Il triste conto di pianti già pianti in abbondanza,

Che di nuovo pago come non fosse mai stato pagato.
Ma se frattanto penso a te, caro amico, tutte
Le perdite son risanate e i dolori hanno fine.

When

When at the call of a tranquil thought
The mind turns to things past, how many voids
You seek among good things as old disgraces
Reappear to waste my fleeting time.

But I do not flood my eyes, I have no use for spilling tears
For friends in the perpetual night of death,
Nor for disgraces in love, long since archived,
Or so many hopes and projects vanished.

So I may torment myself for torments already passed,
And dolefully, disgrace upon disgrace, go over
The wretched bill of sobs already sobbed abundantly,

Which I pay again as though it never had been paid.
But if meanwhile I think of you, dear friend, all
Losses are healed and all pains have their end.

2015

Esodo

dalla finestra vedo piramidali
grigi metronomi a perdita d'occhio
premono argini risalgono colli
                                              discendono su pianure lontane
scandiscono entrate uscite
distendono ritmiche tende sonore.
                L'operaia dall'attaccapanni
                                sceglie fra due vestiti uno lo indossa
                                      si guarda allo specchio:
ineffabile numero
di cellule indivise
                                      ore interminabilmente scandite
aria compressa martello grancassa
metronomi grigi a perdita d'occhio
                                    profitti e perdite e la schiuma
                                    che dalla finestra si vede e avanza
                                            pulsando agli occhi.
Qui solo ieri ragazzo
qui ogni giorno riunisce
                                  forse non guerra ma fughe macerie
                                      della propria casa il cálcare
calcáre polvere di strade straniere
                                            folla infinita follía
                         folla in marcia di gente bimbi a tracolla
                                    sillabano il diurno cammino
                                        sulle acutissime pietre
fra rotaie di ferro
traverse di perfido legno.
                                            Sotto un velo nero
                                    la bimba sorride nel sonno
                                        le troppe frontiere
                                    metronomicamente scandiscono
                                            il poco suo tempo.

Exodus

   … and from your high position
   as far as the eye can see
   grey oil towers
   or is it metronomes
   beat time along river banks
   climb hills give in to the sea

                                you can't know, child,
                   how somewhere else the worker
                                   from her clothesline
                           chooses between two outfits
                           looks at herself in the mirror
                           you can't know, little child,
                       how frozen hospital hours
                         carve out the time of dancing
                             as furious inner clocks beat
                           as trillions of cells subdivide

        grey oil towers time
          usury's slime
           religions unreason
 close your Mediterranean eyes

                              only yesterday unborn
                          to Assyrian nursery rhymes

if hollow is the colour of extinction
on once white complexioned villages
abrasive is the dust of roads
unnatural is war's folly
to mothers' minds

                                        small children
                                   tower on shoulders
                                    of older siblings

Ma se poi
l'uccellino blu e rosso
le vola vicino, la incanta
col non ritmico suo volo,
col suo non ritmico canto.

.

                              who stumble
                        over north-bound trails
                  traipsing over razor-sharp stones
                           between rail tracks

                          past oil-metronomes tick
                                   tock child

    now sleep sleep crossing boundaries
         crushing the longing for bedtime sleep

                 And then!
         The blue-red little autumnal bird
              unexpectedly sings near!
              Wake! You are enchanted
                by the arrhythmic flight
               the compassionate song.

               My sweet little child
                 you have arrived!
                From this aeon on
                 no twisting of life
                no piercing of rocks
              and no other flight out
          but to follow your own lodestar.

2015

Eternal feminine

To Patrizia

You are my orchard and I your fruit and grower.
You are my mother and I your father and lover.
You are my sister and I your son and brother.

Which memories will nurture this last trope?
Which wave disrupt the pond least,
what new lily grow, tenderly in tune
with the memory of one who, oh so soon,
is but a fading glyph in your time of wake,
a frozen flash of light in a now still universe?

Will you clutch this lock of frizzy grey hair
and linger on the runway after take-off,
to take in the ever-widening absence?

It is not in glory I perish nor disgrace,
anchored to your courage, wifemother.

Donne eterni Dei

A Patrizia

Tu sei il mio frutteto ed io tuo frutto e fattore.
Tu sei mia madre ed io tuo padre e amante.
A me tu sei sorella ed io tuo figliolo.

Quale ricordo nutrirà quest'ultimo tropo?
Quale onda disturberà meno lo stagno,
quale ninfea crescerà, teneramente in tono
con la memoria di uno che, oh così presto,
é segno evanescente nella veglia,
scintilla di ricordo nel sogno oramai fermo?

Terrai stretto forse un ciuffo di capelli grigi
e rimarrai un poco sulla pista al decollo,
per assorbire l'assenza in eterno crescente?

Non è in gloria che muoio, nè in disgrazia,
ancorato al tuo coraggio, sposamadre.

2014

Stop listening

Stop listening to your body
if you want to survive the daily grind
of bone over worn bone.
Make wings and fly. Sail. Hear the wind.

Glide over pain closing its path to sound,
gybe, tack and hold miraculously tight
to the gospels that urge calm sea
and safe passage for those calm of mind.

Pain after all is an augur, a drink for the road,
the ransom for your soul,
a door, a swivel that eases that turning point
to peace, that the daily penguin's voice

articulates so clearly just in between the frothing sheets
he shares with us at the Woody Point green marker.
Listen. Listen not in. Listen out.

Smetti d'ascoltare

Smetti d'ascoltare al tuo corpo
se vuoi sopravvivere al macinìo quotidiano
d'ossa sopra ossa consumate.
Fatti ali e vola.

Vai a vela, ascolta il vento,
scivola sopra al dolore
chiudendo il suo sentiero alla mente.
Stramba la randa. Orza e tienti miracolosamente stretto
ai vangeli che incitano calma di mare
e sicuro viaggio a quelli calmi di mente.

Dolore dopo tutto è un augure,
un bicchiere per chi parte,
il riscatto dell'anima,
una porta, una cerniera
che facilita la virata a quella pace,
che la quotidiana voce del pinguino
articola chiara fra lenzuola
di luminosa schiuma
che con noi condivide a Woody Point.
Ascolta. Ascoltati non dentro.

Ascolta l'altro.

2011/16

Tu mi dicesti

Ti chiesi quale strada fosse aperta.
Ancor dicesti 'questa' ed io, mia luce,
fui perso alla intimità di sempre.

Quella che solo morte, mia rugiada,
poteva condurre seco se, al sepolcro,
fu svanita coi venti di settembre,
foglie polvere strida dei cormorani.

Non ci dicemmo altro e l'ultima parola
mi trafisse, disadorna com'era di espressione,
col distacco di chi saluta un morente,
mia gioia, coerente al chiudere le porte

alla noia del giornaliero spegnersi,
nell'odore della separazione imminente,
al canto degli Uccelli qui intorno,
del Paradiso, nel costume nero di galline.

Passò tanto tempo. Anche l'invito 'torna'
gentilmente si spense con la duttilità
della memoria e la flessibilità degli arti.
Rimane l'ansia del perduto, mio amore.

You told me

I asked you which road was open.
Again you told me 'this one' and I, my light,
was last in the intimacy of forever.

The one that only death, my dew,
could only lead with him if, at the tomb,
it vanished with the September winds,
leaves dust cries of the cormorants.

We said no more to one another and the last word
transfixed me, unadorned with expression as it was,
with the detachment of one who greets a dying man,
my joy, in keeping with the closing of the gates

to the tedium of the daily putting out of lights,
in the scent of imminent separation,
to the song of Birds hereabouts,
of Paradise, in the black costume of hens.

Much time passed. Even the call 'come back'
gently went out with the ductility
of memory and the flexibility of arts.
The angst of the lost is what remains, my love.

2017

Primavera

Un'altra primavera.
Un altro aprirsi di finestre e fiori.

Ascolta. Viaggiano meglio i suoni
di qua della frontiera
di tenui bambù. Il rimorchiatore.
La voce della gazza.

Guarda. Tutte le piante
seguono con intenzione
la luce che si attenua
al passeggio di nuvole
cariche di novità
per questo cielo marino.

Guarda ancora.
Platoni volanti
di pellicani bianchi,
cormorani bicolori
e santi navigatori.
Cercano anche riposo.

Senti. Ritorna la sera
ma solo a primavera
aspettano, certi fiori, la luna
per ricominciare
quel guardarsi attorno,
flessuoso più di quanto
si direbbe acconcio
a fiori casti della nuova stagione.

Prega con loro. Di giorno

Springtime

Another springtime.
Another opening
of windows and flowers.

Listen. Sound travels better
this side of lust.
A tugboat.
Bird warbles.

Look. Plants
wilfully follow
light as it fades
clouds passing
heavy with promise
of rain.

Look again.
Flying platoons
of lavish pelicans,
thrifty cormorants,
seafaring saints,
all on the lookout.

Listen. Night is nearing.
Flowers anticipate a full
moon
for looking around.

Pray with them.
As the shadows rise
wake with them
a little while more

sembra un'adorazione
quel cercare di stare
con la corolla fissa
perennemente nella
corona solare.
Al calar della sera
veglia con loro per un poco ancora
e poi smorza ogni luce
per quella lunare.

then yield
each flame
to the full moonlight.

2012

Oltre tanti io, una gente

Dammi ancora una vita partendo da quest'ora
    ed io sarò il poeta, maestro
      della lingua materna che mi sfugge
      e dell'altra ancora da domare.
Dammi ancora più vite ed io sarò quell'uno
    che tutto conosce ed osa ...
    Tutte queste idiozíe peró,
    'fur spesso accennate, mai ben dette'
    in poesia, nel film di quel tale
    i cui giorni si rifanno, identici,
    da ogni nuova alba fino a sera.
Lascia cosí che scambi tutto per un solo pensiero
    che sia nuovo, che si possa dire
      usando parole forse ignote, ma chiare.
Dammi suono che squilli, brioso, e un finale
    per questi versi, nuovo non trito.
    Finale di speranza, finale che è un inizio.
Dammi ancora più vite iniziando da quel punto
    ed io sarò il compositore che si libra
      verso musica magica che dia pace,
      il fisico che inventa un'arma
      disattivante ogni altra senza arbitrio.
Lascia che una folla sia me ed io una folla,
    una gente di settemila milioni, capace
      di riunirci tutti come sé, sorella, fratello
      liberati dai ceppi di essere 'altro.'
Dona a questa moltitudine più vite, fino a che
    si disimparino violenza e carestie,
      rifugio e asilo, ognuno sagace agnello di gregge
      che mantiene i pascoli comuni sempreverdi.

Beyond many I's, one crowd

Give me one more life starting from now
        and I shall be the poet, mastering
        the mother tongue I forget and this
        I still have to master.
Give me even more lives and I will be the one
        who knows and dares …
        All this idiocy, however,
        'oft was thought, but ne'er so well express'd'
        in poems, in the movie of one
        whose days unfold identical
        from each new dawn 'til night.
Let me swap it all for just one original thought
        that is true, that may be said using
        words that can be understood.
Give me fresh sound, rhythm, a ringing close
        for these lines that is not trite.
        A close of hope, a close that's a beginning.
Give me even more lives starting from there
        and I shall be the composer reaching high
        for music magically giving peace,
        the physicist that invents a weapon
        deactivating all others none excluded.
Let a crowd be me and me one crowd,
        one people of seven billion, empowered
        to reunite all as self, sister, brother
        set free of the shackle of being 'other.'
Give this crowd even more lives until our genes
        unlearn violence and famines,
        refuge and asylum, each a clever lamb in a flock
        that shares and keeps the pastures evergreen.

Donaci l'arte del perdono, o tu cui parlo e che non so
    sei la voce, ora solo di rado
    sentita, che quieta e che consola.
Lascia la mente, da tante ora una, che s'apra, s'involi,
    ferma nell'illusione che oltre questa porta
    si aprano di speranza infinibili portali.

Give us forgiveness, you to whom I speak and don't know
      if you are the voice, now so rarely
   heard, that quietens and soothes.
Let the many-in-one mind open up, fly,
      firm in the illusion that beyond this door,
      open never-ending other portals.

2015

Inventario

Se poi io fossi il solo che è rimasto
        vedrei
        ancora un boccaccio
        di vetro spesso
        tre olive verdi
        sentirei l'odore
        di giornale unto
        d'olio e d'inchiostro
forse anche del pane di quei tre pendolari
        trasportati nella piccola
        folla che si muove
        col fruscìo
d'un cespuglio appena sfiorato
        forse
        per non lasciare
        troppi ricordi
        a raggrumarsi
        forti di tempo.
Semplice ogni partenza
        col primo sole
        stanco ogni arrivo
        al costante tramonto
        seguito dalle apparizioni:
        È piccolo lo sciame
        di donne magre
con scope di saggina
        donne di poca voce
        quasi senza rumore.
        Cancellano calme
        i postumi delle nostre presenze
        le briciole
        gli umori
        le buste di plastica

Inventory

Were I to be the last one remaining
    I would see
    a jar
    thick green glasses
    three olives
    I would know the odour
    of newsprint
    oil
    ink
perhaps of loaves half eaten by those commuters
    now huddling
    crowd
    now gliding
    with a soft rustle
bushes brushed by air puffs
    to leave no trace
    to bequeath
    no memory
    that congeals.
Stark each departure
    at daybreak
    weary returns
    constant as sunset
    followed by apparitions:
    small is the swarm
    of wasted women
    with broomcorn brushes
women of hushed self-worth
    calmly they erase
    the shadows of our being
    crumbs
    humors
    plastic bags

la viscosa sostanza del viaggiatore costante
  in quest'ultimo duro
  ma armonioso
  vagone di legno
  della terza classe.
Qual'è il modello eterno che discende
  da queste particelle
  di vero
  non ci è dato
  sapere né ci è dato
  dare significato
a coloro che si muovono di luogo in luogo
  senza
  freno fino al simulacro
  del riposo finale
  il sabato
seguito da un numero chiuso di altri
  giorni
  a gruppi d'illusioni
  a sfoltite chiome
  di alberelli
  di Natale
a chiassi a giochi a cartelle delle tasse
  a funerali
  ad assalti di truppe
  a promozioni a svendite a reclami.
  Fare uno stocktake
  della realtà
  d'un vagone di terza classe
  (tre olive briciole di pane)
  è non meno assurdo

the viscous substance of the constant traveller
        in this hard
        protective
        third-class
        timber carriage
Were I to be the last one remaining
        I might also seek
        some eternal pattern
        descending from these
        particles of truth.
        I might force a reason of being
onto those who move
        from voyage to voyage
waves
        no pause
        up to the allegory
        of a final shore
        —the Sabbath—
followed by a finite number of more
        daybreaks
        flocks of illusions
        dried Christmas trees
        revelries games tax returns
        troopers
        sales puffery build-up
        last offices.
To take stock
        of all that is real
        in this third-class
        railway carriage
        (three olives
        bread crumbs)
        is not less absurd

di fare un inventario
  dell'universo intero.
  O della realtà
  della mente.
  D'una mente
  sola
  racchiusa forse
  ma come su un'isola rocciosa
  il faro

than making an inventory
> of the universe in total
> or the reality
> of mind.
> Of any mind
> alone
> walled in perhaps
> but as on a rocky island
> the lighthouse.

2013

Finire logicamente

Cammina, cammina lento, lento con me
verso la fine del tempo e del sentiero.
Man mano si farà il tuo passo piu leggero.
Tenderai a seguire quegli uccelli in questo
bosco e qui vedrai sparire forme,
le forme che hai racchiuso nella mente.
Non c'è spaziosa radura in fondo al bosco,
né ti offre più natura di sé stessa,
di sé la coltre di vita che rinnova
che pulsa che responde che si schiude.

Cammina, cammina lento, lento con me
verso i giorni finiti, le ore scontate,
i tramonti conchiusi, e le parole
di odio e d'amore confuse in un solo
grande, grande silenzio. C'è il simbolo
dell'infinità del perduto. C'è un solo,
solo pallido passato che non è, pure
essendo. Via, con via, con via, con vita,
convitato, contenuto, continuato.
Significato. Significante. Signifigatto.

Ending logically

Walk, walk slowly, slowly with me
towards the end of time and of the path.
Bit by bit your step will become lighter.
You will be inclined to follow the birds into this
wood and here you will see shapes disappear,
the shapes you have enclosed in your mind.
In the depth of the wood there is no open glade,
nor does it offer you more nature than itself,
it is only the coverlet of life that renews
that pulses that answers that parts open.

Walk, walk slowly, slowly with me
towards the finite days, the numbered hours,
the predetermined sunsets, and the words
of hate and of love commingled in a single
great, great silence. There is the symbol
of the infinity of all that is lost. There is a sole,
sole pale past which is not, and yet
is. Way, with a way, with a way, with a lifetime,
convocated, contained, continued.
Signified. Significant. Significat.

2014

Serenità

La fine dei giorni arriva
attesa con gioia
o con risentimento

scandita da gesti di resa
o di vittoria
dall'ultima foglia vinta
o da quella ora nuova

dal cane che alle cinque
esce rientra e ritrova
la riempita scodella
o non la trova

alternativamente
in alto nuvole chiuse
o ancora più in alto
chi sorride alla mente

ticchettio del cuore
memoria che inizia
accumulo di luce

ma tu non negare
l'attesa clausura
calma cosciente
forse riposo
pace del prima
e, dopo, del dopo

Serenity

The end of days arrives
awaited with joy
or with resentment

underlined with gestures of surrender
or of victory
by the last vanquished leaf
or by the newest one

by the dog which at five o'clock
goes out comes in and finds
the refilled bowl
or does not find it

alternatively
high up closed clouds
or higher yet again
one who smiles at the mind

ticking of the heart
memory that begins
an accumulation of light

but do not deny
seclusion long awaited
calm conscious
rest perhaps
peace of the before
and, after, of the after

2016

Contest

The Mayfly's life can be as short as 30 minutes.
After hatching, she mates, lays eggs and dies.

I shall go before than ...
It started quite young,
at the planting of a sapling:
semper virens said my father.

Years later, the analogy
shifted to the Steinway piano
tropicalized with balsams
to endure austral climes.

When installing an outboard engine,
its life guaranteed to outlast ...
I know, it's rank superstition
but I could not articulate ... *mine.*

Closer to the closing hours,
it's the newly planted cabbage,
garlic bulbs, mignonette lettuce,
raised beds of the vegetable garden.

How shall I compare you now,
inscrutable darling life?
Maybe to the Lady Mayfly
sharing this filtered sunlight?

Gara

La libellula Efemera vive 30 minuti.
Nasce, s'accoppia, figlia e muore.

Me ne andrò io prima.
Ed anche: *Me ne andrò prima di quello.*
Iniziò da bambino
osservando il novissimo arboscello.
Semper virens disse zio Franco.

Anni dopo, a confronto
si pose il nuovo piano tedesco
iniettato di balsami e ormoni
per meglio reggere al viaggio
ed al clima transoceanico.

Un velo di frivola tensione
si formò assai più tardi
con l'arrivo d'un nuovo motore marino
garantito per quarant'anni.
Vivrà quindi più di ... ?
Lo so, è rozza superstizione
ma a me non veniva quel *me*.

Contiguo al tardissimo
tempo di questa cara vita,
termine di misura
è il nuovo cavolfiore,
il bulbo dell'aglio inguattato
sotto il radicchietto rosso.
Nell'orto di casa
sono ben elevate le aiuole.

E domani?
A chi potrò compararti, domani,

celata inscrutabile vita?
Forse con quell'Efemera
che palpita vive muore
nella tepida luce
di quest'ultima stanza?

O forse, buio sopra buio
sullo schermo della mia intima fronte
con le immagini fuggenti
di te, vita cara, gioiosamente
ora quasi del tutto trapassata?

2012

Fork in the road

Sane world impoverished by reason.
Sitting by my cradle, tenderly she thought:
*'Bless, as you don't possess a single word,
no lies for you, nor truth or wisdom.'*

Was there ever a time for a fork in the road,
between futures with, or without
the power to slip away from the silence
of the inner world, into one of words?

Perhaps when the curse of our days,
certainty of death, hadn't yet cast its gloom,
no world would need El Niño, or forest
an arsonist and no name the shadows
that dim our grasp of Nature.
Or should I say, 'Creation?'

Sitting by my cradle, Mammina
still quietly hums *Tu scendi dalle stelle.*
The old tune still needs no words.

2018

For a faraway child

… when time is passing way too fast,
as it happens now at this point of life,
to slow it down place a much loved,
happy child in London or anywhere

that's distant enough to give a sense
of diminishing light, of dust that fell
on once transparent things around,
of a new measure of a world once small,

then receive a message that says:
on this day, on this plane, I shall
arrive, please wait. And you wait

and recall when that child far away
was you. So, like they did, wait
in peace, as this is edged lightly in,

among life's natural burdens …

2017

An age of unsteady progress

For Paolo Totaro

My close friend and I
have reached the Age of Falling,
neither he nor I complaining.
Soon to an Age of Forgetting,
we will, perhaps together,
reach an Age of Reminiscing.
Caught hard on a stair, descending,
by a step somehow missing,
he fell, spent weeks recovering.
His stern eye took in my greeting,
'Whom will write whose Obituary
is not yet settled,' he said, finding
this uncertainty pleasing.

John Bryson (2014)

For John Bryson

John, I wish that you, Fidelio and I
would board a boat that sailed
by willpower alone under kindly stars,
and, with no freak wave or wind.
would take us beyond Good Hope,
serene, and when the sweet dream
of Therese and Pippi necessarily arose,
the glowing clouds would become
stage stairs and, in garden clothes,
majestic the two spouses would climb
down from the Paradise we once shared.
'Or maybe not,' they would quietly say,
finding this uncertainty pleasing.

Paolo Totaro (2014)

Eulogy for Kim Gamble

Now you have been told, Kim,
by superior authority that your time
more or less is up. Less, they said,
and now that I have been also told

by the resident actuary in my genes
that less or more of my time is up
why don't we come to an agreement
to exchange eulogies? We can even

bargain as to what each will say.
I promise truth. In short, that
you made two wholesome girls,
had an amazing lover and a talent
for inventing gnomes, and drawing
out of branches, sea, red walls
and pieces of timber, magic
paintings. Like me, you also had,
I shall say, that self-same inducement
to self-destruct, kept at bay for
as long as it took, also to build love
as well as other ingredients
that make time worth of being lived.

That my eulogy will contain even less
words, Kim, I won't guarantee neither
dryness of eyes or steady
voice, reflecting on the size
of an immense loss.

2015

The race

we check early in the morning
we check we aren't dead
we aren't object of tears to shed
as yet and on so hearing we forget
which was more feared his or mine
I mean the death.

                    Personally I wouldn't mind
to go first and leave him the honour
of my eulogy but in a church which poses
an intractable problem as he never tires
to say that organized r and priests
to speak not of him up there, up,
are only worthy of a laugh and there
is no laugh in a prayer.

                            With my ball
of fat a cyst behind the right ear
and my stoop, my tremor and drip
who will leave first will take the memory
of the golden hair the sandals stippled
for the other to remember those times
just after WWII and the runs up and down
in front of her and her school and the spoken
gazes and the scorns and the purple
paraments of the passing coach with
four black horses.

                    Be my guest, have the
grey ashes, they will be mine and so will
the echo of voices out of open mouths.

2012

Delayed clarity

… it happens these days that any word
is weighed, before trusting it to sound,
explored for density, for potential
to rise or rile or be replaced again
by stillness within, around.

Articulate implies an artistry.
Like gathering flowers or shedding
light maybe through enigmas
treated as delayed clarity
or invitations to wait for sunbreak

as this early bird's song breaks into the silence
of a new day, after the long night's
quietly imagined nightingale song
and you turn for one more hour of sleep …

2008

The architect's gene

In memoriam Harry Seidler

The home this mouse built, for herself, mate and brood
is a tunnel, complex, to you and me a pinhole in the ground.
Over there, clay, saliva, dung, the termites' mound scrapes
their sky. Green tree-ants sew their home in a leaf, one design.

Weaverbirds aerial nests, of chewed grass and palm leaves,
pulse against the sunlight. Yes, living things all have innate
sense of roof, of eaves. They don't boast. Don't add
to the palimpsest, humbly react to what is internally told.

Humans, however, Pheidías to Seidler, improve on ancestors:
towers, domes, each add to the great predecessors,
build homes great as theatres and theatrical places to rest,

try to move one step, two step higher the originality
ladder. Their works may last longer. But all living creatures'
nests do not outlast time. Or man's other gene. For war.

2015

Ave atque vale

For Jeremy Steele

We met only a few times. Yet Jeremy
is in the heart a close friend now lost.
Anne, the caring Anne, made us meet,
mature men linked by an illness of the soul.

He said: 'Is only this what defines a man?'
Because his true trait was hugeness of love
enriched by guilt, he then also said:
'I can't plan for long vacations, as I see

in diminishing stretches good weather.'
He truly was a luminous intellect,
his own lightning rod, his own shield

for his children and the woman he loved.
A towering man longing for infinity,
patrician Jeremy, hail and farewell.

2014

Ecce gratum

Another opening
of flowers and windows.
Listen. Sound travels better
this side of lust.
A tugboat.
Bird warbles.

Look. Plants
wilfully follow
light as it fades
clouds going past
returning
heavy with promise
for sky
their inquisitive master.
God I want to die.

Look again.
Flying platoons
lavish pelicans
thrifty cormorants
seafaring saints
all on the lookout.

Please god let me die.
The little boy's cry
In our living room.

Pray with him
in full daylight
it will seem
to adore

that staying spellbound
as corollas
in the coronal
sunlight

The punch of a dwarf child
live on tv as he wakes
to his achondroplasia.
Shadows
in our living room
do not meet.

Now think about.
Night is nearing.
At springtime
flowers wait for a full moon,
to begin
that looking around
more alluring than
proper
for a chastity bloom.

As the shadows rise
wake for them
a little while more
then yield
each flame
each gene
to a full moonlight.
Hope is you, child.

2020

Pygmalion

Even the sculptor could not cope
with the hugeness of her ambition.
While other statues daren't dream
to hatch out of their stone prison,
she alone decided to moon-dance
in Michael Jackson's sinuous motions.

Likewise, if you are in my time of slowing,
when poetic rivers are caught between
the two states of water and ice,
don't groan: poems need only a dream
to hatch out of their frozen prison.
So, free the full rainbow of passions,

scream how *old* is just another mould
to break, scream one more poem
in jarring rhyme for whomever cannot hear,
encased in coma or palliative care,
until all words end in the silence of ashes.
Oh Pygmalion, don't blunt your chisel just yet.

There is time still.

2014

After the deluge

After us, not the deluge
but a light rain
over millennia
will eagerly wash
earth of the concrete
sky of the noise of jets
sea of man the fisher.

New shoots quickly grow
green through the marble paving.
Tendrils spread
along bank columns.
Foundation-breaking roots
envelop the mega-cities,
digest the slum
and the architectural
concept.

Fungi feast on paper money.
Crews of mega-ants
huge dragonflies
powerful scarabs
work night and day
until every trace
is wiped away.

Twisting over the eons,
the orbit of the planets
will bring Titan and Pluto
closer to the Sun.
Their ice lands will melt
new oceans will grow

new rain. The same
forces that made us alive
will be at play again.
Titan will be concreted
and Pluto fished out.
New coins minted.
Titanic architects
will build.
Plutonic forces
will destroy.
Eons will run their course.
After them, not the deluge
but a light rain …

2014

Open the door

A tribal birthday

Open the door right now as the time
of opening doors is streaming out.

Don't go around.
Don't go aimlessly around with dreamy eyes:
It will endear you only to those who dream
dreams of mountains already climbed.

And that's alright if you're ready,
if you're ready to give up before completing
Your trial. Yes, you, you dear one with the cell phone,
Hiding to longing, veiled looks

Of those you are shutting out.
See past the sinisterness that fills the ether:
There is a truer truth waiting for you,
you grandchild, but also for other humans

in wait …
      … for what?
           … to be called
                  … healed back to full life?

Now listen to your heart, and to the trees
and birds whose flesh you won't eat.
In the far distance there will be a call:
The music of the spheres, for when

all other noise is crossed out.
But listen more, my child. That's a long,
long way from where you sit,
where you now sit in the faraway wonders

of the not fully fought out. A nearer call
to health of body and spirit:
The time to heed is now
as all around you, your tribe is cheering:

Welcome back! ....sorpresa qui

2021/ 2023

The quest

… when time goes faster I walk more slow
don't count the daily pops as pills quit
their silvery blister, ignore all other clocks:
the bell tower dong, the birds' early call,

pull in my head as turtlets do when cold
don't look don't listen don't feel the prick
of agin-bite re-morse, confession, forgive
me father, padre pardòn, forgive the sense

that we never healed after we were born,
death each raindrop, gifted ghost
of a second past, that won't lay ahead
at any time to come, and light was as

on day one, and then a cockcrow and then
for all time to go, was it now or long ago,
forward, hereafter, hereinafter, day out day in,
first slow now faster than any speed I know …

2017

Sombrement

… what she'll see, after you're dead,
is some grief, even tears
along with callers with not
much to say, one at a time,

clothes that gradually disappear
from closets while others will appear,
gender fluid, countenanced,
so that she may move

towards brighter colours:
floral, aquamarine, non-severe
chemises, pantaloons.
But in the fridge, alone,

our old box of *confetti*,
those of the wedding kind
white in the original box
finger smeared by time

as it slowly passes them by …

2020

Last prayer

… imagine the last second of the very last minute
and, in it, the closing thought: I see your face
sculpted not in marble but in streams
of mountain water,
in the light mist that closes this wintertime

in the pink cloud that heralds
the timeless night,
in this flash that extinguishes thought.
You are.

You do not guide and are not guided. You are no further
from me than me, nor as elusive as another's mind.
And as this day

will not fade into another, I know you cannot be good
or evil. You are. You are the vessel of the serene idea
that imparts meaning to planets and stars,
to the parliament of men and to my children,
and to this raw flesh

that is your creation. Yet, it is not your grace that eludes
but our will. And this is what I feel
and that in this last second of the endmost minute
I must let go. The time to be at peace with you has now begun …

2013

Notes

p. 9: 'First time at the cinema ...'

James Whale's 1931 famous horror film, *Frankenstein*, based on Mary Wollstonecraft Shelley's 1818 novel, was known to me since my father took me to see it in 1943. Soon after, I read a shortened Italian version of Mary Shelley's book that, unlike the film, ended with the escape and pursuit of the Creature to the North Pole. My friend and I were allowed to go to see the film at the Diana Cinema near our homes in Naples, in 1944. The Brothers Grimms'/ Disney's cartoon film *Snow White and the Seven Dwarfs* (1937) was in that same year dubbed in Italian as *Biancaneve e i Sette Nani*. It could be seen in Italy's cinemas during WWII years, notwithstanding the fact that it was an enemy-made movie. I still have two books on the film, dated 1938. Incidentally, Biancaneve's song in the woods, birds dancing with her, was dubbed by great soprano Lina Pagliughi. The names of the seven diamond-mining brother dwarfs became in Italian Dotto, Mammolo, Pisolo, Gongolo, Eolo, Brontolo and Cucciolo (Doc, Bashful, Sleepy, Dopey, Sneezy, Grumpy, Happy) and are still known to Italian children as such, eighty-three years after the film and two hundred years after the original German.

p. 15: 'Baronìa d'acquisto / Peerage for sale'

biribissi: a traditional Italian gambling game, similar to roulette, played for low stakes.

p. 46: 'Empires'

In the First Italo-Ethiopian War, 1895-1896, Ethiopia's military victory over Italy secured it the distinction of being the only African nation to successfully resist European colonialism. Ethiopia at the time was called Abyssinia in the common European parlance. On March 25, 1889, the Shewa ruler Menelik II—having conquered Tigray and Amhara—declared himself Emperor of Ethiopia. Barely a month later, on May 2, he signed a treaty of amity with the Italians, which apparently gave them control over Eritrea, the Red Sea coast to the northeast of Ethiopia, in return for recognition of Menelik's rule. Menelik II prolonged the policy of the Tewodros II about integration of Ethiopia. However, the bilingual Treaty of Wuchale did not say the same thing in Italian and Amharic. The former text established an Italian protectorate over Ethiopia, which Menelik discovered soon afterwards. The Amharic version, however, merely stated that Menelik could contact foreign powers and conduct foreign affairs through Italy if he so chose. Italian diplomats, however, claimed that the original Amharic text included the clause and Menelik knowingly signed a modified copy of the Treaty. Because of the Ethiopian refusal to abide by the Italian version of the treaty and despite economic handicaps at home, the Italian government decided on a military solution to force Ethiopia to abide by the Italian version of the treaty. In doing so, they believed that they could exploit divisions within Ethiopia and rely on tactical and technological superiority to offset any inferiority in numbers. The Second Italo–Abyssinian War (also referred to as the Second Italo-Ethiopian War or just the Ethiopian War, Italian: *Guerra d'Etiopia*) was a colonial war that started in October 1935 and ended in May 1936. The war was fought between the armed forces of the Kingdom of Italy (*Regno d'Italia*) and the armed forces of the Ethiopian Empire. The war resulted in the military occupation of Ethiopia and its annexation into the newly created colony of Italian East Africa (*Africa Orientale Italiana*, or AOI). Politically, the war is best remembered for exposing the inherent weakness of the League of Nations. Like the Mukden Incident in 1931 (the Japanese annexation of three Chinese provinces), the Abyssinia Crisis in 1935 is often seen as a clear example of the ineffectiveness of the League. Both Italy and Ethiopia were member nations and yet the League was unable to control Italy or to protect Ethiopia when Italy clearly violated the League's own Article X. The positive outcome of the war for the Italians coincided with the zenith of the international popularity of dictator Benito Mussolini's Fascist regime, in a phase called 'the age of consensus' during which foreign leaders praised him for his achievements. Historians like James Burgwyn called the victory of Mussolini 'a capital achievement,' but he was forced to accept the Anschluss between Nazi Germany and Austria, and to begin a political tilt toward Germany that finally destroyed him and Fascist Italy in World War II. Indeed this Italian victory, that brought about the Italian Empire with Ethiopia included, was short-lived as Ethiopia regained its independence only five years later during World War II at the end of the East African Campaign with the help of Allied forces.

p. 63: 'Gods' obituary'

De Rerum Naturae: ('On the Nature of Things,' 1st century BC) is a poem by the Roman poet and philosopher Lucretius (c 99 BC—c 55 BC). He wrote about the tragedy of human nature against superstition.

p.83: 'Runaway bride'

The Bride of Christ is the Church, the community of believers.

p. 85: 'Sentinel'

In Greek mythology, Talos was an *automaton,* a giant of bronze who protected the nymph Europa in Crete from invaders. He circled the island's shores three times daily. The Bendix RIM-8 *Talos* was a long-range naval surface-to-air missile, among the earliest carried by United States Navy ships.

p. 101: 'The art of self-deprecation'

'Lettres de cachet'—Royal sentence without appeal.
'Chateau d'If'—The island-prison into which Dumas' Count of Monte Cristo was thrown.

p. 102: 'And foundering is sweet in such a sea'

'The Infinite,' in *Canti* by Giacomo Leopardi, translated from the Italian and annotated by Jonathan Galassi, Farrar, Straus and Giroux, 498 pp. Original Italian, 'L'Infinito,' *Canti*, B.U.R. Milano, 1949. *Sempre caro mi fu quest'ermo colle, / e questa siepe, che da tanta parte / dell'ultimo orizzonte il guardo esclude. / Ma sedendo e mirando, interminati / spazi di là da quella, e sovrumani / silenzi, e profondissima quïete / io nel pensier mi fingo, ove per poco / il cor non si spaura. E come il vento / odo stormir tra queste piante, io quello / infinito silenzio a questa voce / vo comparando: e mi sovvien l'eterno, / e le morte stagioni, e la presente / e viva, e il suon di lei. Così tra questa / immensità s'annega il pensier mio: / e il naufragar m'è dolce in questo mare.* Translation by Jonathan Galassi: *This lonely hill was always dear to me, / and this hedgerow, which cuts off the view / of so much of the last horizon / But sitting here and gazing, I can see / beyond, in my mind's eye, unending spaces, / and superhuman silences, / and depthless calm ,/ till what I feel / is almost fear. And when I hear / the wind stir in these branches, I begin / comparing that endless stillness with this noise: / and the eternal comes to mind, / and the dead seasons, and the present / living one, and how it sounds. / So my mind sinks in this immensity: / and foundering is sweet in such a sea.* Regarding my poem's first line, 'My Mum taught me to rhyme and count syllables': in Italian poetry, metre is determined solely by the position of the last accent in a line, the position of the other accents being important, however, for verse equilibrium.

p. 103: 'You asked me'

In Plato's Allegory of the Cave, prisoners who know no other reality, watch shadows of objects passing in front of a fire that cast light on the walls of their cave. For them, the human condition is forever bound to the impressions received through the senses. Even if these are an absurd misrepresentation of reality, we cannot break free from the bonds of our human condition—a *phenomenal* state—just as the prisoners could not free themselves from their chains. If, however, we were to miraculously escape our bondage, we would encounter a higher reality than the one we have always known: the realm of pure *Form* and pure *Fact*.

p. 112: 'Fence sitters'

'Coloro / che visser sanza 'nfamia e sanza lodo' (Dante Alighieri, *Inferno*, III, 35-36). Dante finds himself in the circle of the Inferno to which are relegated the souls of those who never took a side and who lived without infamy or commendation.

p. 115: 'Space semiotics'

Is there a new kind of ruling class, and could we view it as one that mostly controls information? It's really not interested in things; it doesn't directly own factories. It doesn't care about the meaning of words. It cares about controlling the value chain through controlling information. There are elements of that all through capitalism, but for it to be emerging to the point of dominance is relatively new.

p. 116 Image by Paolo Totaro.

p. 136: 'A wailing sonnet'

The place the poet and Osky, a neighbour's dog, inhabit is likened to a theatre set. But a window has been ripped open in the theatre set canvas, here meaning a death. The dead dog was half-dingo. Litigious, yet loved by his owner and friends. Old age, for the poet and the dog, was the best time of their life. What was the dog's story? Why is he dead now? Would the dog have chosen to be euthanized? The poet leaves unexpressed what he would wish for himself. As a dog, Osky couldn't speak. Perhaps he didn't need to, as he was free of men's illusion that they must utter words, no matter how dull.

p. 166: 'Carpe Diem in Balmain'

The fact that the poet was inspired by Alcaeus here is unimportant; this conception of life and time, justly famous, is connected with Horace and the extraordinary economy with which he expressed the following:

> Tu ne quaesieris, scire nefas, quem mihi, quem tibi
> finem di dederint, Leuconoe, nec Babylonios
> temptaris numeros. Ut melius, quidquid erit, pati,
> seu plures hiemes, seu tribuit Iuppiter ultimam,
> quae nunc oppositis debilitat pumicibus mare
> Tyrrhenum: sapias, vina liques, et spatio brevi
> spem longam reseces. Dum loquimur, fugerit invida
> aetas: carpe diem, quam minimum credula postero.

p. 188: 'The gift of fire'

An additional reflection—

> It could not have been *High Noon*, but it was one of the many Westerns
> we would go and see around 2pm at our nearby Cinema.
> The feeling of revulsion we had for some of the Allied Forces soldiers in our streets—
> as children on the threshold to adolescence, we saw, understood, grieved the
> corrupting influence of the invaders on a shell-shocked population—bombings,
> devastation, German occupation, Fascist stupidity, broken down rules of living together.
> And there seemed to be no lasting evasion going to the movies. Not anymore.

p. 218: 'Ulysses'

Regarding the dedication to Dante: in the *Inferno*, Dante found that Ulysses had committed three offences: devising and executing the stratagem of the wooden horse; luring Achilles into the war effort (for which Achilles abandoned Deidamia and their son); and stealing the Palladium—a statue of Athena which protected the city of Troy—with the help of a Trojan traitor, Antenor (*Inf.* 26.58-63). Note the famous speech to his companions, to keep on going beyond the columns of Hercules: 'Considerate la vostra semenza: fatti non foste a viver come bruti, ma per seguir virtute e canoscenza.' Regarding the dedication to Tennyson: Tennyson had his Ulysses speak these words:

> It little profits that an idle king,
> By this still hearth, among these barren crags,
> Match'd with an aged wife, I mete and dole
> Unequal laws unto a savage race,
> That hoard and sleep, and feed, and know not me.
> I cannot rest from travel: I will drink
> Life to the lees: …
> … We are not now that strength which in old days
> Moved heaven and earth; that which we are, we are;
> One equal temper of heroic hearts,
> Made weak by time and fate, but strong in will
> To strive, to seek, to find, and not to yield.

p. 222: 'Esodo / Exodus'

Oil wells are misuse of space, Nature. Metronomes are manipulation of time. Exodus is dislocation in time and space.

p. 236: 'Oltre tanti io, una gente / Beyond many I's, one crowd'

See St Thomas Aquinas, *Summa Theologiae*, Ia Q. 39 Art. 8.
'oft was thought, but ne'er so well express'd'—Alexander Pope, *An Essay on Criticism* (1711)

p. 262: 'Ecce gratum'

'Ecce gratum (primo vere)' ('Behold, the pleasant spring') was the title of a students' poem written early in the 13th century, as part of the *Carmina Burana*. Set to music in 1935-36 by German composer Carl Orff. Only the title is borrowed in this poem.

p. 264: 'Pygmalion'

This is my interpretation of the story of Pygmalion the Cypriot sculptor. In Ovid, Pygmalion kisses Galatea, a ravishing sculpture he has made and finds her lips warm, touches her and finds her soft and damp: Aphrodite had granted Galatea her wish to break out of her stone prison and be a woman and Pygmalion his wish to have a wife. In my poem, the prisoner is an old man who wants to break out of his mould. Maybe poetry will allow him to do it albeit in the secret of his mind?

Translations by

Paolo Totaro

Un sogno / A dream
Cinque giornate/ Five days (Second day)
Capire / To know
A gentle answer / Una calma risposta
Disimparare / Unlearning
Miti sinistri / Universal logic
Come Lui li volle / As He wanted
Parola e Logos / Word and Logos
The birth of myths / Il nascere dei miti
Pittwater
Le colline dormono ormai / The hills are now asleep
Carpe diem a Balmain / Carpe diem in Balmain
The new Pope / Il nuovo Papa
Cena domenicale / Sunday dinner
Mail stone
Esodo / Exodus:
Eternal feminine / Donne eterni Dei
Stop listening / Smetti d'ascoltare
Primavera / Springtime
Gara / Contest
Oltre tanti io, una gente / Beyond many I's, one crowd
Inventario / Inventory
Serenità / Serenity

Theodore Ell

Baronìa d'acquisto / Peerage for sale
Cinque giornate / Five days (First, Third, Fourth and Fifth days)
Il primo Ulisse / The first Ulysses
Immaginario / Imaginary
Antiche bombe e il Coronavirus / Ancient bombs and the Coronavirus
Mandela
Come di sera d'estate / As on a summer's evening
Un regalo gradito / A gift appreciated
L'arte del conversare / The art of conversation
Quando / When
Tu mi dicesti / You told me
Finire logicamente / Ending logically

Paolo Totaro was born in Naples in 1933. He studied at the Jesuit-run Il Pontano, after which he went to both the Conservatorio San Pietro a Majella, where he graduated in pianoforte, and to the Università Federico II, where he gradiated in law. He worked in the international department of Fiat, which led to his transfer to Sydney in 1963, with his young family. In 1975, the family decided to remain in Australia, as Paolo had been invited to join the Australia Council as the first Director of Community Arts. In 1977, he was appointed the founding Chair of the New South Wales Ethnic Affairs Commission. He served in that position until 1989 as well as writing for *The Bulletin* and presenting the SBS television program *Face The Press*. In later years, he became a Visiting Professor at the University of Western Sydney and Pro-Chancellor at the University of Technology, Sydney. As well as continuing to perform as a pianist, for most of his life Paolo has written poetry in English and Italian. He became known particularly for his contemplations of the migrant experience and of the landscape and seascape of Pittwater, north of Sydney, which has been his main home in Australia. His *Collected Poems (1950-2011)* were published in 2012.

Theodore Ell is a writer, translator and Honorary Lecturer in literature at the Australian National University in Canberra. Ell's poetry collection *Beginning in Sight* shared the 2022 Anne Elder Award, and he won the 2021 Calibre Essay Prize for 'Façades of Lebanon,' his account of surviving the 2020 Beirut port explosion. His memoir of the full two years he spent living in Beirut, *Lebanon Days*, was published in 2024. From 2012 to 2015 he was co-editor of *Contrappasso Magazine*. Ell's poetry, essays and translations have been published in Australia, the UK, Italy and Lebanon. He is writing a new authorised biography of Australian poet Les Murray.

Alice Loda is a Lecturer in International Studies and Global Societies at the University of Technology, Sydney. Her research sits at the intersection of cultural studies, migration studies, literary theory and aesthetics. Her most recent work addresses transcultural poetry in contemporary Italy and Australia, with a focus on form and environment.

www.ingramcontent.com/pod-product-compliance
Lightning Source LLC
Chambersburg PA
CBHW020518080526
44583CB00013B/646